Re-Designing the High School Library
for the Forgotten Half

Re-Designing the High School Library for the Forgotten Half

The Information Needs of the Non-College Bound Student

MARGIE J. KLINK THOMAS

LIBRARIES UNLIMITED
U N L I M I T E D
A Member of the Greenwood Publishing Group
Westport, Connecticut • London

Library of Congress Cataloging-in-Publication Data

Thomas, Margie J. Klink.
  Re-designing the high school library for the forgotten half : the information needs of the non-college bound student /
Margie J. Klink Thomas.
    p. cm.
  Includes bibliographical references and index.
  ISBN 978-1-59158-476-6 (alk. paper)
  1. High school libraries—United States. 2. Vocational education—United States. 3. High schools—Curricula—United States. 4. School librarian participation in curriculum planning—United States. 5. Educational change—United States. I. Title.
  Z675.S3T47 2008
  027.8′223—dc22   2008014019

British Library Cataloguing in Publication Data is available.

Library of Congress Catalog Card Number: 2008014019
ISBN: 978-1-59158-476-6

First published in 2008

Libraries Unlimited, 88 Post Road West, Westport, CT 06881
A Member of the Greenwood Publishing Group, Inc.
www.lu.com

Printed in the United States of America

The paper used in this book complies with the
Permanent Paper Standard issued by the National
Information Standards Organization (Z39.48–1984).

10 9 8 7 6 5 4 3 2 1

Contents

Acknowledgments

To Dean Paskoff and faculty at the School of Library and Information Science at Louisiana State University.

Special thanks to Nicholas A. Gish, for his unstinting efforts in fact checking, formatting, and footnoting.

My interest in the information needs of non-college bound students began soon after I accepted the position of Librarian at the then new West Valley High School in Fairbanks, Alaska. The furniture was in place, the collection was growing, students were appearing in great numbers to do research and find 'reading for interest' material. I was networking and collaborating with the Advanced Placement and academic teachers to ensure that the collection was reflecting the needs of the curriculum and their particular classes and teaching styles. Then, one day, Virgil Thayer came into the library. Virgil, a quiet, gentle man who taught 'metals' (welding), asked me pleasantly, "Can my kids use this library?"

It was at that point that it became clear to me that, even in our relatively affluent school, located just down the hill from the university where many of our students' parents taught or were employed, a good number of students would not be continuing their education in a formal sense immediately after high school. While most of our students would graduate, the option or opportunity for pursuing a college degree was not immediately possible. The military, technical or business school, or immediate entry into the workforce presented attractive alternatives to the classroom for many. In fact, our school, like many others, roughly fit the national statistical profile: 85–90% of our students would complete high school, but fewer than 25% of those would complete a college degree.

Thanks to Mr. Thayer's query, I began to look again at the library's collection, services, and overall program, and realized that there was little to reflect the needs or interests of that non-college bound student—the kid who wanted to be an A&P (Air Frame and Power Plant—aircraft) mechanic, or pipeline welder, or professional musician. My interest and concern—and my research—continues to the present. Thank you, Virgil Thayer, to opening my eyes to the needs of the Forgotten Half.

1

High School Re-Design, Restructure, and Reform in the 20th Century

"The society which scorns excellence in plumbing as a humble activity and tolerates shoddiness in philosophy because it is an exalted activity will have neither good plumbing nor good philosophy ... neither its pipes nor its theories will hold water."

John W. Gardner (1912–2002)

When Mary A. Kingsbury began her work as the librarian at Erasmus Hall High School in Brooklyn, New York, in June 1900, she was the first of about 50 trained librarians named to high schools between 1900 and 1915. Erasmus Hall had been a famous private school since its founding in 1787. When Ms. Kingsbury began her work there (at $600.00 per annum), the collection boasted about 650 volumes, including a rare copy of Samuel Johnson's *Dictionary* (Clark 1951, 50–51) among other volumes.

The high school library at Erasmus Hall High School consisted of a box-like room with shelves reaching to the ceiling (see Clark 1951, 50, for photograph). The collection was "academic" in nature, since Erasmus Hall had been a prestigious college preparatory academy up until the time it was turned over to the city of New York for use as a public high school. Though collections of books in schools suitable for the age and interests of the participants were not new—the idea had been promoted for 50 to 60 years—Ms. Kingsbury, a graduate of the library program at Pratt Institute, represented a new breed. She had been a classroom teacher (Greek, Latin, and German) and was inspired to attend Pratt Institute in 1898, where, upon completing the program, she was lauded as being "the most brilliant member of the most brilliant class ever to be graduated from Pratt," according to Mary Plummer, head of the Pratt Library School at that time (Clark 1951, 50). Ms. Kingsbury spent the year following graduation working as a cataloger, before accepting the position at Erasmus Hall.

Many of the school library collections and services at that time had sprung from the local public library movement, and were viewed as "branches" of those public libraries. They were generally maintained on site by an interested teacher in the school, and, in some instances, the collections consisted of old textbooks, or classic literature from another era. The concept of developing a "library program" for high school students, with material that was new and pertinent and relevant to their interests, a library program that related to the educational curriculum and to the academic and career and vocational interests of the students, was still in its nascent stage in 1900, but developed rapidly as more and more education systems across the country saw fit to hire their own professionally trained librarians. Mary Kingsbury and those who came after her in the following 10 to 15 years oversaw the development of a philosophy of school library services that continues with us today.[1]

The development of school library programs and collections that spoke to "vocational guidance," to providing material and support and encouragement for all students, began to evolve about the time of Mary's appointment, as it became clear to educators and librarians that only a very few of the students at that time would be going to college. Most would be joining the workforce upon high school completion, if they completed high school, and about 85 percent of them did not (U.S. Department of Commerce—Bureau of the Census—Historical Statistics of the United States).

In 1913, Marilla Waite Freeman, the librarian at Goodwyn Institute Library in Memphis, Tennessee, wrote an article published in the April 1913 *Library Journal* (Freeman 1913, 179–83) titled, "The Joint Work of the High School and the Public Library in Relating Education to Life," a treatise in which Ms. Freeman advocated an increased presence of vocational advisors in high schools, and the much-needed attention of the high school librarian in selecting and purchasing material for the school library that would be of value to students in selecting and preparing for career employment. (Recommended titles included *Vocations for the Trained Woman: Opportunities Other than Teaching*, 1910; and *Vocations for Boys*, n.d.) A few years later, E. L. Cook wrote an article for the *Bulletin of the American Library Association* (1922, vol. 16) on the "relation of the high school librarian to the technology and manual training departments," in which she wrote, " ... It is possible for the librarian and teacher working together to develop a very consistent use of technical books." Ms. Cook later writes, in the same article, " ... The librarian must be thoroughly acquainted with the kinds of courses given in the school, and with their arrangements, since much depends upon a good understanding of the correlation of these courses. Then she should be well grounded in the best books on these subjects in order that she may be able to characterize them briefly for reference purposes. Of course, the work which actually counts is the continuous search for new books, pamphlet and magazine material, though it is most important that no purchases should be made without consulting the teachers for whose classes the material is intended" (Cook 1922).

The history of Career Technical Education (CTE) in the 20th century provides something of a philosophical parallel to that of the development of school library programs. Both became recognized components of public education at the beginning of the 20th century. Both recognized the need for high school coursework and material that would allow young people to move into employment following high school. However, the academic curriculum in high schools tended to remain patterned after the curriculum and structure and course of studies in universities. When practical courses were introduced in the high school, they were increasingly relegated to a kind of second tier, many times requiring less academic preparation and fewer rigorous standards. The impact of national legislation and funding for CTE and curricular models that stress the integration of academic theory and practical skills application of theory has resulted in both positive and negative results for many of the nation's high schools.

In 2003, Michael E. Wonacott published *History and Evolution of Vocational and Career-Technical Education* for the Center on Education and Training for Employment (Wonacott 2003, ED482359). The purpose of his paper (compilation, as he terms it) was " ... to sketch the evolution of the field from vocational education to career-technical through the course of a century of practice in public school systems in the United States." Thus, the paper is a compilation of information and excerpts from a variety of sources, including both original and foundational documents from the early 20th century and more recent histories and syntheses from the end of the century. An emphasis is given to early foundation documents by Snedden, Prosser, and Dewey, which set the course for a century of vocational education and which wittingly or unwittingly anticipate issues that underlie the reconceptualization of vocational education in the last decades of the 20th century (Wonacott 2003, 1).

Mr. Wonacott's work relies on a variety of books, scholarly publications, and reports for background for the paper, including that of David Snedden (at that time Commissioner of Education for Massachusetts), *The Problem of Vocational Education* (1910). Snedden observed that the demise of institutions like the home, the farm. and apprenticeship, coupled with the rise of public education (including more plentiful libraries) and the increasing influence of the press, was providing for three broad types of education for different purposes (Wonacott 2003, 3–4):

- ✧ **Physical education** was intended "to produce and preserve bodily efficiency, such as health, strength, and working power."

- ✧ **Vocational education** was intended "to promote the capacity to earn a living, or, expressed in more social terms, the capacity to do one's share of the productive work of the world."

- ✧ **Liberal education** "contributed ... to the improvement of social life and to the development of personal culture to fit the individual to live among his fellows."

Snedden (according to Wonacott) further divided vocational education into areas based on the occupations for which individuals were prepared:

- ✧ **Professional education** prepared lawyers, doctors, engineers, teachers, clergy, and the military.
- ✧ **Commercial education** prepared bookkeepers, clerks, stenographers, and business leaders.
- ✧ **Industrial education** prepared bricklayers, machinists, shoemakers, metal workers, factory hands, and others in manufacturing.
- ✧ **Agricultural education** was designed to prepare individuals "looking to the tillage of the soil and the management of domestic animals" (Wonacott 2003, 9).
- ✧ **Education in the household arts** prepared girls for dressmaking, cooking, and management of the home.

Snedden noted later on in his work that vocational education was provided at public expense, through public education to "those unfortunates—delinquents, dependents, and defectives—for whom the home no longer exists ... because liberal education left the individual unprepared for the practical affairs of life" (Wonacott 2003, 12). Snedden was particularly concerned about the vocational education of African Americans, in that he felt it would or could serve as groundwork for liberal education (Wonacott 2003, 13).

Only a few years later, John Dewey wrote that public education should develop in youth the continued capacity for growth, the lifelong ability to continue learning. He criticized educators who:

> ... imposed their own personal aims on education—to lead youth to read classic literature instead of pulp fiction, for example. Such externally imposed aims, divorced from learners' present reality and activities, amounted to preparation for a future that was entirely remote and disconnected from daily life and led to learning and teaching that were rote, mechanical, and slavish. (Dewey 1916, 144)

Dewey advocated, among other things:

- ✧ Building on individuals' interests to develop discipline (Dewey 1916, 162)
- ✧ Connecting experience and thinking, not separating them into separate phases
- ✧ Providing learners the opportunity to produce "good habits of thinking" (Dewey 1916, 192)
- ✧ Teaching that focuses not on the details of the subject matter but on the characteristics of the learner
- ✧ Subject matter with worth not for its own sake but for the ability of individuals to incorporate it into daily life and activities

✧ Education that taps into a student's natural interests and transforms it into intrinsically motivated work

Dewey contended that education in a democratic society " ... must do away with the dualism of a 'liberal education' having to do with ... [a] life of leisure devoted to knowing for its own sake, and ... practical training for mechanical occupations, devoid of intellectual content ... and instead construct a course of studies which makes thought a guide ..." (Dewey 1916, 305).

Wonacott also quotes R. L. Lynch (2000) on the Smith-Hughes Act (P.L. 64-347) of 1917: " ... It was enacted to prepare youth for jobs resulting from the industrial revolution and to provide them with an alternative to the general curriculum of schools, which were too exclusively literary in spirit, scope, and methods" (Swanson 1951, 16).

The Smith-Hughes Act of 1917 was the first of several pieces of federal legislation that provided funding for vocational/technical education directly from the U.S. Congress to state departments of education. (The current iteration is Perkins IV—Carl D. Perkins Career and Technical Education Improvement Act of 2006 [Public Law 109-270].) Smith-Hughes was solely for the use of vocational or technical education; however, it tended to increase the separation between academic and vocational curriculum. Vocational teachers emphasized job-specific skills in their courses, sometimes nearly to the exclusion of any theoretical content. So, though carpenters and electricians certainly required increasing mathematics and literacy skills, those were taught separately, in the academic side of the curriculum. And, in all too many instances, students who were deemed to be unable to cope with a more academic curriculum were tracked into vocational courses requiring little academic preparation. That situation is changing, however.

While federal money continues to be directed specifically to vocational and technical education, business education, special needs students, and those in economically depressed communities and stand-alone vocational-technical institutions are treated differently. The education reform movements are increasingly calling for a greater level of integration of academic skills into CTE courses, and a greater level of collaboration between CTE and academic teachers.

Education Reform

"The forgotten half" is a term first used in a 1988 report from the W. T. Grant Foundation Commission on Work, Family and Citizenship. It refers to those high school students who will either not attend or not complete college. The 1988 report pointed out the vast imbalance in public investment between those who attend college and those who do not. The term, coined more than 20 years ago, continues to reverberate. However, researchers continue to document that "only 70% of all students in public high schools graduate, and only 32% of all students leave high school qualified to attend four-year colleges" (Greene and Forster 2003). The year

2000 report from the U.S. Bureau of the Census indicates that some 80.4 percent of Americans over the age of 25 indicated that they had a high school diploma or higher, and 24.4 percent of the same population, Americans over the age of 25, indicated that they had a bachelor's degree or higher (U.S. Census Bureau 2000).

Note that Greene and Forster (above) is referring to students in public high schools and that the Census Bureau is measuring or counting self-reporting by all Americans, including those who have a diploma from a private high school. Public schools are obligated to educate all students who come to them, and private schools have the option of being more selective, admitting those students most likely to complete the diploma requirements and those who will cause the least disruptions.

In public schools, the triage system seems to be used frequently, though not openly nor with any acknowledgment. Triage, from the French meaning "to sort," is a commonly used medical system of evaluating the extent of medical care required by patients, usually in emergency or trauma situations. Patients are divided into 3 to 4 tiers, based upon the need for immediate medical attention in order for the patient to survive. For instance, Tier 1 may be those patients who have no chance to survive; Tier 2 may be those who must receive immediate attention or they will perish; Tier 3 might indicate patients who need attention, but whose medical condition is not immediately life-threatening, and therefore care might be postponed; Tier 4 could be cases in which the patient has slight injury, but who will survive regardless of whether or not he/she receives medical attention.

Applied to the education community, Tiers 1 and 2 have much in common. These represent students who have learning, physical, emotional, or social disabilities that will almost certainly mean that high school completion will require immediate and costly attention for that child to succeed, if at all. Students with disabilities and students at risk are certainly worth our education system's attention; and, in most cases, education systems across the country do everything in their power to address those special needs students by providing specialized materials and equipment, special programs, smaller classes, tutors, and so on in order for those students to excel to the greatest extent possible. It is possible that these students collectively represent as much as 25 percent of the total.

Likewise, Tier 4 students, those on Advanced Placement, honors, and college prep tracks, will almost certainly succeed. They will complete high school and college, and in many instances continue their educations in graduate or professional programs. They represent perhaps 25 percent of our students, and again, our educational dollars are well spent ensuring that they work with the best teachers, the smallest classes, and the best and newest equipment, technology, and resources. These students will succeed, and they will be our doctors and attorneys and scientists and researchers and librarians.

And that leaves Tier 3, the "forgotten half" representing about 50 percent of our students who almost certainly attend public high schools, and who almost certainly take few if any Advanced Placement or International Baccalaureate or honors classes. They are placed in regular or general track classes with 30 or more of their peers. These are the students who will serve in our nation's armed forces, who will drive the huge trucks on our nation's highways, who will, in fact, build and maintain those highways. They will pilot aircraft and trains and boats and ships. They will construct buildings and regulate complex electronic monitoring systems in our factories and industrial complexes. They will be our police officers and paramedics and firefighters and rescue workers. They will manage our food industry and much of our health care system. They will keep our financial and personnel records straight and play major roles in our hospitality and entertainment industries. They must develop strong skills in high school because for many the opportunity for a two- or four-year college degree or technical school diploma is not an immediate realistic option.

One of the "bibles" of employment is the *Occupational Outlook Handbook*. The 2006–2007 edition (accessed online 14 July 2006) reports that:

- ✧ "About 3 out of every 10 new jobs created in the U.S. economy will be in either the healthcare and social assistance or private educational services sectors.... Healthcare and social assistance ... will grow by 30.3 percent and add 4.3 million new jobs (2004–2014 period)."

- ✧ "Professional and business services ... will grow by 27.8 percent and add more than 4.5 million new jobs.... The fastest growing industry in this sector will be employment services, which will grow by 45.5 percent and will contribute almost two-thirds of all new jobs in administrative and support and waste management and remediation services. Employment in professional, scientific, and technical services will grow by 28.4 percent and add 1.9 million new jobs by 2014. Employment in computer systems design and related services will grow by 39.5 percent.... Employment growth will be driven by the increasing reliance of business on information technology and ... maintaining system and network security."

- ✧ "Information ... expected to increase by 11.6 percent ... contains some of the fast-growing computer-related industries such as software publishers, Internet publishing and broadcasting, Internet service providers, Web search portals, and data processing services."

- ✧ "Leisure and hospitality ... will grow by 17.7 percent. Arts, entertainment and recreation will grow by 25 percent ... by 2014. Most of these new job openings will come from the amusement, gambling and recreation sector.... Accommodation and food services is expected to grow by 16.5 percent ... [and] will be concentrated in food services and drinking places."

- ✧ "Trade, transportation, and utilities ... will grow by 10.3 percent ... [led by] truck transportation and warehousing. Employment in retail trade is expected to increase by 11 percent. Employment in water, sewage and other systems is expected to increase 21 percent."

- ✧ "Financial activities ... real estate and rental and leasing is expected to grow by 16.0 percent.... The fastest growing industry [in this super-sector] ... will be activities related to real estate.

[Other areas of growth] will be … finance and insurance, securities, commodity contracts, and other financial investments."

✧ "Government … including public education and hospitals, is expected to increase by 10 percent."

What, exactly, do these jobs require, and what does education reform have to do with it?

Various studies, blue ribbon commissions, reports, and books have been published in the past 50 years demanding changes in the public education system in the United States.

James Bryant Conant's 1959 best-seller *The American High School Today: A First Report to Interested Citizens* was not the earliest examination of U.S. high school public education, but represents a good starting place for a couple of reasons. John W. Gardner, president of the Carnegie Corporation of New York, wrote, in the foreword to Conant's book, that it was an examination of "some of the critical problems facing the American high school" (Conant 1959, ix). He further noted that Conant did not invent the concept that became the comprehensive high school; he simply endorsed the obvious and made suggestions for its improvement. The comprehensive high school had evolved to meet the needs of the increasing number of 20th-century students who perceived that a high school education was requisite to a good job. In the foreword to the book, Gardner describes this phenomenon:

> It is called comprehensive because it offers, under one administration and under one roof (or series of roofs), secondary education for almost all the high school age children of one town or neighborhood. It is responsible for educating the boy who will be an atomic scientist and the girl who will marry at eighteen; the prospective captain of a ship and the future captain of industry. It is responsible for educating the bright and the not so bright children with different vocational and professional ambitions and with various motivations. It is responsible, in sum, for providing good and appropriate education, both academic and vocational, for all young people within a democratic environment which the American people believe serves the principles they cherish. (Conant 1959, ix)

Idealistic, not politically correct, and perhaps never fully realized, the term "comprehensive high school" nonetheless served as a model for hundreds of communities across the nation. Conant, in fact, described the evolution of the so-called comprehensive high school by tracing its roots to the American ideals of equality of opportunity and equality of status; the urge for institutional expansion on the part of colleges and universities; and finally, to child labor laws prohibiting the employment of youth (Conant 1959, 7). The idea of the comprehensive high school is disintegrating, however, as communities realize that the concept is no longer valid for today's students. In fact, National Public Radio's *Morning Edition* on Wednesday, April 11, 2007, featured a story on Northwestern High School in Baltimore, Maryland, which, like many other "comprehensive high schools" is a "a dinosaur." Local officials are making plans to "shrink" the school, to develop a more personalized learning and technologically appropriate educational experience (http://www.npr.org/templates/story/story.php?storyId=9485120).

Twenty-five years after Conant, *A Nation at Risk* (National Commission on Excellence in Education [NCEE] 1984) noted that "the educational foundations of our society are presently being eroded by a rising tide of mediocrity that threatens our very future as a Nation and a people" (NCEE 1984, 5) and that " ... individuals in our society who do not possess the levels of skill, literacy, and training to this new era will be effectively disenfranchised ..." (NCEE 1984, 7). *A Nation at Risk* listed 14 "Indicators of Risk." Stated among these indicators, business and the military were " ... required to spend millions of dollars on costly remedial education and training programs in such basic skills as reading, writing, spelling and computation" (NCEE 1984, 6–7). "Computers and computer-controlled equipment are penetrating every aspect of our lives ..." (NCEE 1984, 10). "Technology is radically transforming a host of ... occupations. They include health care, medical science, energy production, food processing, construction, and the building, repair and maintenance of sophisticated scientific, educational, military, and industrial equipment" (NCEE 1984, 10). The commission found that the "cafeteria style curriculum" of high schools permitted students to migrate "from vocational and college preparatory programs to 'general track' courses in large numbers" (NCEE 1984, 18). "Twenty-five percent of the credits earned by general track high school students are in physical and health education, work experience outside the school, remedial English and mathematics, and personal service and development courses, such as training for adulthood and marriage" (NCEE 1984, 19).

Other works critical of the American system of education published in the 1980s included: *A Place Called School* (Goodlad 2004), *Horace's Compromise* (Sizer 2004), and *The Shopping Mall High School* (Powell 1986). The executive summary to *Workforce 2000: Work and Workers for the 21st Century* (1987) says that "students must go to school longer, study more, and pass more difficult tests covering more advanced subject matter. There is no excuse for vocational programs that 'warehouse' students who perform poorly in academic subjects or for diplomas that register nothing more than years of school attendance" (Johnston 1987, 6).

The 1991 SCANS Report (U.S. Department of Labor, Secretary's Commission on Acquiring Necessary Skills) identified five competencies and a three-part foundation necessary for workplace know-how, or "solid job performance" (Hudelson 1992, xviii):

FIVE COMPETENCIES

Resources	Identifies, organizes, plans, and allocates resources
Interpersonal Skills	Works with others
Information	Acquires and uses information
Systems	Understands complex inter-relationships
Technology	Works with a variety of technologies

THREE-PART FOUNDATION

Basic Skills	Reads, writes, performs arithmetic and mathematical operations, listens and speaks
Thinking Skills	Thinks creatively, makes decisions, solves problems, visualizes, knows how to learn, and reasons
Personal Qualities	Displays responsibility, self-esteem, social-ability, self-management, and integrity and honesty

America 2000: An Educational Strategy (1991) defined itself as "a national strategy, not a federal program.... It recognizes that real education reform happens community by community, school by school, and only when people come to understand what they must do for themselves and their children and set about to do it" (*America 2000* 1991, 11–12).

Popular publications of the 1990s also recognized and pointed out inadequate preparation for the workplace. Kathryn and Ross Petras, in 1990's book *Jobs '90: Leads on More than 40 Million Jobs and How to Get Them*, write about the

> ... growing shortage of trained employees for U.S. business. The baby boom is over, and there are fewer young, educated employees for American business. At the same time, skills are declining in technical areas as well as general areas. It is not unusual for entry-level bankers to be required to study business writing and communications; this problem is common up and down the corporate and government employment ladder, and is worse for technical positions. (Petras and Petras 1990, viii)

A recently published study and critique of the U.S. public education system is *Tough Choices or Tough Times: The Report of the New Commission on the Skills of the American Workforce,* issued by the National Center on Education and the Economy (December 2006). A summary of the 169-page report is available at www.skillscommission.org/study.htm. The report urges vast changes in the nation's education system to ensure success in the workforce of the future and the competitiveness of American workers in an international economy. In addition to advocating that all students should have or develop strong skills in English, mathematics, technology and science, literature, history and the arts, it stresses the requirement for developing critical thinking, the ability to analyze and synthesize data, self-discipline, innovation, creativity, flexibility, and problem-solving as being the essential skills for the future. The study calls for a thorough re-vamping of K–12 education, with particular emphasis on moving school governance, policymaking, and funding from the local to the state level.

Note

1. Other school librarians appointed about that period of time were Mary E. Hall, Girls' High School, Brooklyn, New York, appointed 1903; Bertha Hathaway, Morris High School, New York City, appointed 1903; Celia Houghton, Albany High

School, appointed 1905; Mary Groves, East High School, Rochester, New York, appointed 1905 (Hall 1915, 627).

References

Abramson, Larry. "Tales from Northwestern High: Troubled Schools Turn Around by Shrinking." http://www.npr.org/templates/story/story.php?storyId=9485120 (accessed 11 April 2007).

America 2000: An Education Strategy. Washington, DC: United States Department of Education, 1991.

A Nation at Risk. Washington, DC: National Commission of Excellence in Education, 1983.

Carl D. Perkins Vocational and Applied Technology Education Amendments of 1998. Public Law 105-332. (ED429191).

Clark, Maude B. "Mary A. Kingsbury, Pioneer." *Wilson Library Journal* 26 (September 1951): 50–51.

Conant, James Bryant. *The American High School: A First Report to Interested Citizens,* 1st ed. New York: McGraw-Hill, 1959.

Cook, E. L. "Relation of the High School Librarian to the Technology and Manual Training Departments." *The Bulletin of the American Library Association* 16 (1922).

Dewey, John. *Democracy and Education: An Introduction to the Philosophy of Education.* New York: Free Press, 1916.

Freeman, Marilla Waite. "The Joint Work of the High School and the Public Library in Relating Education to Life." *The Library Journal* 38 (April 1913): 179–83.

Goodlad, John I. *A Place Called School.* McGraw-Hill: New York, 2004.

Greene, Jay P., and Greg Forster. *Public High School Graduation and College Readiness Rates in the United States.* Education Working Paper .3, New York: Center for Civic Innovation at the Manhattan Institute, 2003.

Hall, Mary E. "The Development of the Modern High School Library." *Library Journal* 40 (September 1915): 627.

Hudelson, Dale. *SCANS: Roadmap to the Future: A Summary of the Interim and the Final Report of the Secretary's Commission on Achieving Necessary Skills, with Background Analysis.* Alexandria, VA: American Vocational Association, 1992.

Johnston, William B. *Workforce 2000: Work and Workers for the 21st Century.* Indianapolis, IN: Hudson Institute, 1987.

Lynch, R. L. "New Directions for High School Career and Technical Education in the 21st Century." Information Series No. 384. Columbus: ERIC Clearinghouse on Adult, Career and Vocational Education, Ohio State University, 2000.

National Center on Education and the Economy. *Tough Choices or Tough Times: The Report of the New Commission on the Skills of the American Workforce.* December 2006. http://www.skillscommission.org/study.htm.

National Commission on Excellence in Education. *A Nation at Risk: The Full Account*. United States Government: Washington, DC, 1984.

Petras, Kathryn, and Ross Petras. *Jobs '90*. 1st ed. New York: Prentice Hall Press, 1990.

Powell, Arthur G., Eleanor Farrar, and David K. Cohen. *The Shopping Mall High School: Winners and Losers in the Educational Marketplace*. Boston: Houghton Mifflin, 1986.

Sizer, Theodore R. *Horace's Compromise: The Dilemma of the American High School*. New York: Houghton Mifflin, 2004.

Snedden, David. *The Problem of Vocational Education*. Boston: Houghton Mifflin, 1910.

Swanson, J. C., comp. *Development of Federal Legislation for Vocational Education*. Chicago: American Technical Society, 1951.

United States Bureau of Labor Statistics. *Occupational Outlook Handbook*. Washington, D.C.: United States Department of Labor, 2006. (Accessed 14 July 2006).

United States Census 2000. http://www.census.gov.

U.S. Department of Education Center for Education Statistics. Digest of Education Statistics: 2007. Table 8.

Wonacott, Michael E. *History and Evolution of Vocational and Career-Technical Education*. (ED 482359). Columbus: Center on Education and Training for Employment, College of Education, Ohio State University, 2003.

2
Models for Reform and Re-Design: Where's the Library?

"Every reform was once private opinion."

Ralph Waldo Emerson

The effort to re-design, or reform, the way high schools work, the manner in which the public education systems in the states and throughout the nation attempt to revamp themselves to hold the attention of and train and educate today's students for further education and the workplace has resulted in a variety of networks, models, and thought. This chapter will review a few of the examples of these reform models being used and advocated.

Partnership for 21st Century Skills

The Partnership for 21st Century Skills, http://www.21stcenturyskills.org, serves as something of an "umbrella" to define and explain the rationale for the need for these reform efforts. The American Association of School Librarians (AASL) has joined this effort because the Partnership does address the need for and value of information and media literacy and research, in other words, strong, well-developed school library media programs. The Partnership for 21st Century Skills is a tax-exempt 501(c)3 organization. The Partnership's work is supported by the U.S. Department of Education.

What is the Partnership?

The Partnership for 21st Century Skills has emerged as the leading advocacy organization focused on infusing 21st-century skills into education. The organization brings together the business community, education leaders, and policymakers to define a powerful vision for 21st-century education and to ensure that students emerge from our schools with the skills needed to be effective citizens, workers, and leaders in the 21st century.

Framework for 21st-Century Learning

The Partnership's framework for learning in the 21st century is based on the essential skills that our children need to succeed as citizens and workers in the 21st century. The Partnership has identified six key elements of a 21st-century education, which are described below. An overview of the framework and the Partnership can be accessed at http://www.21stcenturyskills.org.

1. **Core Subjects**. The No Child Left Behind Act of 2001, which reauthorizes the Elementary and Secondary Education Act of 1965, identifies the core subjects as English, reading, or language arts; mathematics; science; foreign languages; civics; government; economics; arts; history; and geography.

2. **21st-Century Content**. Several significant, emerging content areas are critical to success in communities and workplaces. These content areas typically are not emphasized in schools today:

    ✧ Global awareness

    ✧ Financial, economic, business, and entrepreneurial literacy

    ✧ Civic literacy

    ✧ Health and wellness awareness

3. **Learning and Thinking Skills**. As much as students need to learn academic content, they also need to know how to keep learning—and make effective and innovative use of what they know—throughout their lives. Learning and thinking skills are comprised of:

    ✧ Critical thinking and problem-solving skills

    ✧ Communication skills

    ✧ Creativity and innovation skills

    ✧ Collaboration skills

    ✧ Information and media literacy skills

    ✧ Contextual learning skills

4. **ICT Literacy**. Information and communications technology (ICT) literacy is the ability to use technology to develop 21st-century content knowledge and skills, in support of 21st-century teaching and learning.

5. **Life Skills**. Good teachers have always incorporated life skills into their pedagogy. The challenge today is to incorporate these essential skills into schools deliberately, strategically, and broadly. Life skills include:

   ✧ Leadership

   ✧ Ethics

   ✧ Accountability

   ✧ Adaptability

   ✧ Personal productivity

   ✧ Personal responsibility

   ✧ People skills

   ✧ Self-direction

   ✧ Social responsibility

6. **21st-Century Assessments**. Authentic 21st-century assessments are the essential foundation of a 21st-century education. Assessments must measure all five results that matter—core subjects; 21st-century content; learning skills; ICT literacy; and life skills. To be effective, sustainable, and affordable, assessments must use modern technologies to increase efficiency and timeliness. Standardized tests alone can measure only a few of the important skills and knowledge students should learn. A balance of assessments, including high-quality standardized testing along with effective classroom assessments, offers students a powerful way to master the content and skills central to success.

While the Partnership for 21st Century Skills encapsulates much of the thought and many of the ideas being discussed and written about, it was preceded by some of the following papers and reports.

The U.S. Secretary of Education's High School Leadership Summit sponsored by the Office of Vocational and Adult Education (October 2003), available at http://www.ed.gov/about/offices/list/ovae/pi/hsinit/index.html, provided some overview of recent concerns and criticisms, and suggested methods of addressing those concerns. The report mentioned in part that some of the approximately 16,000 U.S. high schools are in greater need than others. The report estimates that 6 to 12 percent of American high schools are "deeply troubled institutions that need major transformations." Many of these schools are concentrated in high-poverty communities, though by no means all. The report further notes the need for re-evaluating high school expectations.

> ... Virtually all American high schools need a dramatic re-evaluation of their expectations. The schools we have today were never created with an eye toward establishing a high level of academic expectations for all students. Regardless of how they may have changed their graduation requirements over the last 20 years, most large comprehensive high schools, the kind that serve about 70 percent of American youth, have never seriously

addressed the way they track students into vocational, general or "college prep" paths, offering different expectations and curricula for different students. Fewer still have then taken the next step and planned varying degrees of programmatic change and staff development that are aligned with heightened expectations. (Cites Brady 2003)

In addition to the call for re-evaluating high school expectations, the High School Leadership Summit also directed investigation into state and district policies, the size (student population) of high schools, and the necessity for providing higher quality instruction in high schools. The Summit identified what was termed "Noteworthy Networks."

Noteworthy Networks

To create entire high schools based on high expectations for all is extremely challenging, particularly for schools where large percentages of students are being tracked toward lower expectations. The following networks and foundations have been noted for improving performance for large numbers of students:

Carnegie Corporation High School Initiatives (www.carnegie.org/sub/program/national_program.html [accessed 4 June 2008])

The Carnegie Corporation.

Because the expansion of educational opportunity is inextricably linked to the revitalization of democracy, we are integrating our Education and Strengthening U.S. Democracy programs into a unified National Program and focusing our grantmaking on two major goals:

1. **Creating Pathways to Educational and Economic Opportunity**—generating systemic change across a K–12 continuum, with particular emphasis on secondary and higher education, to enable many more students, including historically underserved populations and immigrants, to achieve academic success and perform with the high levels of creative, scientific and technical knowledge and skill needed to compete in a global economy.

2. **Creating Pathways to Citizenship, Civil Participation and Civic Integration in a Pluralistic Society**—increasing integration of immigrants into American society through civic education and citizenship and increasing tolerance through education about immigrant cultures. This goal encompasses broadening understanding of democratic institutions and pluralism while strengthening civic education to prepare young people to live in a complex society and contribute to a vibrant democracy in the United States.

In furthering these goals, the National Program will build on efforts already in place in support of teacher education, school reform, literacy and immigrant integration. Grantmaking activities will include support of demonstration programs, promising innovations and capacity-building in selected institutions as well as research, communications, policy analysis and advocacy.

Gates Foundation (www.gatesfoundation.org/UnitedStates/ Education/TransformingHighSchools/ModelSchools.htm [accessed 4 June 2008])

The Gates Foundation likewise supports education, research and reform. The Foundation notes support for "Model High Schools," grouped in three general categories: Traditional, theme-based, and student-centered. Specific examples of these models were located at www.gatesfoundation.org/ UnitedStates/Education/TransformingHighSchools/ModelSchools and include:

Traditional
These schools teach traditional subjects but focus on rigorously preparing every student for college or work.

✧ Aspire Public Schools

✧ Coalition of Essential Schools

✧ The College Board Schools

✧ Cristo Rey Schools

✧ Early College High Schools

✧ Institute for Student Achievement

✧ Knowledge Is Power Program (KIPP)

✧ National Council of La Raza Charter School Development Initiative

✧ New Schools Venture Fund

✧ Replications Inc.

Theme-based
These schools organize coursework around a theme—such as the sciences, technology, or the arts—to engage student in a college-prep curriculum.

✧ Asia Society

✧ Envision Schools

✧ Expeditionary Learning Schools

✧ High Tech High Schools

✧ New Technology High Schools

Student-centered

These schools create individualized plans for each student, often with student input and may focus especially on dropouts or at-risk youth.

✧ Communities in Schools

✧ Diploma Plus/Center for Youth Development and Education

✧ Gates-EdVisions Project

✧ Maya Angelou Public Charter School/See Forever Foundation

✧ The Metropolitan Regional Career and Technical Institute (The Met)/The Big Picture Schools

✧ National Association of Street Schools

✧ YouthBuild USA National Schools Initiative

Schools Making Progress (http://www.sedl.org/slc and http://www.nwrel.org/scpd/sslc/descriptions/index.asp)

"Schools Making Progress is a Web-based and print series that highlights Smaller Learning Communities (SLC) grantee schools making considerable progress on the SLC front. The [individual] school descriptions provide resources and ideas to other schools interested in creating their own SLCs.... Approaches vary from one school to another, but all of the schools use one or more of the structures and strategies (below) that help a school attain the benefits of an SLC." Detailed information on SLC structures, strategies, and grant funding is available at the U.S. Department of Education (www.ed.gov/print/programs/slcp/index.html) website and through the 2001 publication "New Small Learning Communities: Findings from Recent Literature" at http://www3.scasd.org/small_schools/nlsc.pdf.

Structures	Strategies
✧ Academics	✧ Freshman Transition Activities
✧ House Plans	✧ Multi-year Groups
✧ School-Within-a-School	✧ Alternative Scheduling
✧ Magnet Schools	✧ Adult Advocate Systems
	✧ Teacher Advisory Systems
	✧ Academic Teaming

Model Programs

While the networks identified above look at consortia of schools, the model programs are designed to be implemented on a building by building basis. The High School Leadership Summit found the following programs of particular interest. While not all of these model programs have large amounts of research yet to support their effectiveness, each addresses a different set of circumstances that can impair achievement. The American Association of School Administrators (AASA) has also produced a directory of these and other comprehensive school reform models that identifies the available evidence on their successes. The directory, *An Educators' Guide to Schoolwide Reform* (1999), is available at www.aasa.org/issues_and_insights/district_organization/Reform/approach.htm.

- ◇ Initiated by the Southern Regional Education Board, **High Schools That Work** (http://www.sreb.org/programs/hstw/hstwindex.asp) has worked with documented success to help more than 1,200 sites in 32 participating states (2007) turn around low-performing high schools by improving curriculum and instruction.

- ◇ Developed by Johns Hopkins University's Center for Research on Students Placed at Risk, the **Talent Development High School** (http://www.mdrc.org/project_29_17.html) reform model divides large, urban high schools into smaller units ("academies"), including a Ninth Grade Success Academy and academies based on career themes for students in the upper grades.

- ◇ **First Things First** (www.irre.org/ftf/) is a K–12 reform model developed by the Institute for Research and Reform in Education that is supporting widespread reforms in Kansas City, Kansas; Houston, Texas; Shaw, Mississippi; and other communities.

- ◇ **Expeditionary Learning Outward Bound** (http://www.elob.org/) engages students in "expeditions" consisting of cooperative learning projects that integrate content from different subjects, such as mathematics, language arts, social studies, and art.

- ◇ **Modern Red SchoolHouse** (http://www.mrsh.org/) individualizes student progress through different educational levels (as opposed to conventional grades), while using the Core Knowledge curriculum.

The Northwest Regional Education Laboratory (NWREL) likewise maintains a "catalog" of school reform models and initiatives at www.nwrel.org/scpd/catalog/modellist.asp with links to each of the models listed.

All of these education reform initiatives, networks, and models developed to date have agreed on a number of points:

- ◇ A good portion of the system *is* (and perhaps has been) broken, and needs fixing, because many school districts adhere to an older education model that is not working for today's students in today's world.

- ◇ Networks and models are consistent in recommending the need to address a number of other points:
  - ◇ Literacy
  - ◇ Higher academic standards for all students
  - ◇ Stronger hands-on/applied programs for non-college bound students

- ◇ Smaller school units
- ◇ Collaboration among teachers
- ◇ Community support
- ◇ Inclusion and integration of the use of technology
- ◇ Staff training (professional development)—note: this is what the model programs sell, literally, if they are hired to bring about changes in a high school program

These model plans for revamping education do not generally address the inclusion of strong school library media centers, with their potential wealth of print and non-print information and strong teacher librarians. The exception is the "umbrella" Partnership for 21st Century Skills. In researching the literature and news reports, neither states nor school districts necessarily adopt any of these program models outright. Consequently, it becomes necessary for school library media specialists to become familiar with the high school reform scenarios in their individual states, in order to develop strategies to implement information and media literacy skills instruction into all academic and career areas of the curriculum of our high schools.

In order for the school librarian to move with confidence into high school re-design, particularly as it addresses the needs of the "forgotten half," it is a good idea to become familiar with the CTE literature and agenda.

References

American Institutes for Research. *An Educators Guide to Schoolwide Reform.* 1999. http://www.aasa.org/issues_and_insights/district_organization/Reform/approach.htm.

Bill and Melinda Gates Foundation. "Gates Foundation National District and Networks Grants Program and Related High School Initiatives." http://www.gatesfoundation.org/Education/SmallHighSchools/RelatedInfo/Evaluation NationalSDNetworkGrantsProg-030421 (accessed 4 June 2008).

Brady, R. "Can Failing Schools be Fixed?" Thomas B. Fordham Foundation, 2003. http://www.edexcellent.net/library/failingschools/failingschools.html.

Carnegie Corporation of New York. "Carnegie Corporation High School Initiatives." http://www.carnegie.org/sub/program/education.html (accessed 4 June 2008).

"Expeditionary Learning Outward Bound." http://www.elschools.org/.

"High School Leadership Summit." October 2003. http://www.ed.gov/about/offices/list/ovae/pi/hsinit/index (accessed 18 August 2006).

Institute for Research and Reform in Education. "First Things First." http://www.irre.org/ftf.

MDRC. "Talent Development High School." 2007. http://www.mdrc.org/project_29_17.html.

Modern Red SchoolHouse Institute. "Modern Red SchoolHouse." 2005. http://www.mrsh.org/.

National Center on Education and the Economy. "Tough Choices or Tough Times: The Report of the New Commission on the Skills of the American Workforce." December 2006. http://www.skillscommission.org/study.htm.

Northwest Regional Educational Laboratory. "Schools Making Progress Series." 2002. http://www.nwrel.org/scpd/sslc/descriptions/index.asp.

"Partnership for 21st Century Skills." 2004. http://www.21centuryskills.org.

Southern Regional Education Board. "High Schools That Work." 1999. http://www.sreb.org/programs/hstw/hstwindex.asp.

U.S. Department of Education. "Smaller Learning Communities Awards Database." 2006. http://slcprogram.ed.gov/.

3
Collaborating with the CTE Faculty: Research and Application

"It seems clear that many of the difficulties that people experience throughout their lives are closely connected with beliefs they hold about themselves and their place in the world in which they live. Students' academic failures in basic subjects, as well as the misdirected motivation and lack of commitment often characteristic of the underachiever, the dropout, the student labeled "at risk," and the socially disabled, are in good measure the consequence of, or certainly exacerbated by, the beliefs that students develop about themselves and about their ability to exercise a measure of control over their environments."

Frank Pajares, *Schooling America: Myths, Mixed Messages, and Good Intentions*

Few researchers have examined high school library media centers and their use by or effect upon the vocational education curriculum. Dorin's (1960) study reported the paucity of work done to that time, noting that literature in the field was limited to "masters' theses, articles in professional publications, and occasional reports to library associations" (Dorin 1960, 13).

Manikas (1981) studied the shop collections in two-year vocational technical programs, comparing them to the schools' libraries as they related to the vocational-technical instruction program. She found that faculty considered the library's holdings in their subject areas less adequate, and placed less importance on the use of library materials to expand course content, believing that materials housed in the library would receive more use if they were located in the classrooms or shop areas. She suggested that better cooperation was needed between faculty and librarians for delivery of library media services (Manikas 1981, 119). Manikas also discussed work published to that time on the use of library media resources and materials by vocational education programs, including Dorin's (1960) study and a master's thesis by Welsh (1949) dealing with library resources for high schools serving vocational education students, as well as a number of journal articles published from 1926 to the mid-1970s (Dorin 1960, 19–39).

The journal articles primarily dealt with the establishment and use of school libraries in high school vocational programs, and were limited to articles such as that published by the North Carolina State Department of Instruction's "Advisory List of Instructional Media for Vocational Education" (North Carolina State Department of Public Instruction 1977 and 1978).

A technical report by Parrott et al. (1982) from the College of the Sequoias, *Vocational Students' and Instructors' Perceptions and Usage of COS Library Services*, found that 88 percent of the 226 students surveyed in business, industry, technology, and nursing felt comfortable in libraries, 84 percent enjoyed reading, 55 percent indicated that their friends frequently used the library, 76 percent learned to use the library in high school, and 64 percent felt that libraries have information that is helpful to carpenters, welders, electricians, and mechanics. Business students agreed more strongly with the statement that their instructors felt library use was important. The 37 vocational faculty members surveyed were making minimal to moderate use of the library, and though 73 percent of the faculty members indicated that they encouraged their students to use the library, they did not require it.

Peifly (1981) used school library, audio-visual aids, and teaching supply expenditures as one of a number of means of analyzing "the delivery of vocational education in New Jersey" (abstract), but found only that "local finance sources proved highly sensitive to shifts in funding commitments at state and federal levels," with no indication as to the role, if any, of library media resources.

Thomas (2000) found that in three comprehensive high schools in Florida, there was little knowledge on the part of the CTE faculty of library media center resources, and little interest on the part of the school library media specialist in the CTE programs. The exception to this was noted by a building trades CTE instructor. He enthusiastically explained that in the career academy (one of six in his school), in which he was teamed with academic teachers, those teachers took pains to find out what he was working on in order to sculpt their units around it. He gave the example of a unit he had done on constructing trusses for roof structures in buildings of any type. The social studies and English teachers worked with these same students to research and write about the use of trusses in buildings from ancient times to the present, the variations in materials that were used, major innovations and when they occurred, and a developing awareness of current materials and methods used in constructing trusses. While the CTE teacher made no mention of the use of material or services from the library media center, it is not difficult to see ways in which the library media specialist could and should be involved here.

Classroom teachers (as noted by Parrott et al. above) strongly influence student use of school libraries. Ducat (1960), Blazek (1971), Hartley (1980), Burks (1993), among others, all examined teacher influence on student use of the school library. Hartley noted that teacher preparation programs rarely include any direction to pre-service teachers of the availability and use of library media services and resources or the advantages of working cooperatively with the school librarian (1980, 127). Burks concluded that teachers play an important role in influencing students to use library facilities and resources, but that many teachers were unaware of the value of library materials in their subject teaching areas. She further noted that librarians and teachers needed to strengthen their lines of communications, and that librarians must do a better job of promoting the resources and services available in their facilities (Burks 1993, abstract).

What Matters Most: Teaching for America's Future (1996) developed three simple premises for teacher preparation programs:

⬦ What teachers know and can do is the most important influence on what students learn.

⬦ Recruiting, preparing, and retaining good teachers is the central strategy for improving our schools.

⬦ School reform cannot succeed unless it focuses on creating the conditions in which teachers can teach, and teach well.

The school library research community continually advocates the integration of research or information literacy skills throughout the school curriculum, as well as collaboration and cooperation with classroom teachers in teaching students in all areas awareness and use of materials and resources pertinent to that teacher's area of specialization. However, recent and rapid changes in school programs and curricula, the impact of computers and telecommunications upon education, the lack of funding for technology and other resources, and classroom teachers who are themselves unaware and untrained in the use of library media materials and technologies seemingly continue to stymie progress, particularly among those students of "the forgotten half."

School Libraries Work! (2006) tells us in a loud, clear voice that well-funded, professionally staffed school libraries can positively impact student academic achievement. Based on studies completed in 19 states, it succinctly describes each of those studies, with additional reference to papers and articles from national publications and agencies, including No Child Left Behind (NCLB), the National Commission on Libraries and Information Science (NCLIS), the International Reading Association (IRA), the American Library Association (ALA), researchers including Blanche Woolls, and the New York State Education Department.

While each of the above noted 19 state studies completed to date vary somewhat in their approach, methodology, and focus, the overall message is clear. School libraries with well-prepared, certified school library media specialists, with reasonable funding for both print and non-print collection development, with effort made to work positively and collaboratively with classroom teachers and administrators, help students to succeed academically.

The Association for Career and Technical Education (ACTE) issued a position statement on high school reform in January 2006, titled *Reinventing the American High School for the 21st Century: Strengthening a New Vision for the American High School through the Experiences and Resources of Career and Technical Education*. The paper provides research and rationale for including CTE opportunities within high schools "re-designing" themselves, noting that more than 95 percent of high school students take at least one CTE course, and nearly one-third complete three or more related CTE courses before they graduate. Agreeing with premises by the networks and models for school reform noted in chapter 2, ACTE suggests a threefold purpose of career and technical education in secondary schools:

◇ Support students in the acquisition of rigorous core knowledge, skills, habits, and attitudes needed for success in postsecondary education and the high-skilled workplace;

◇ Engage students in specific career-related learning experiences that equip them to make well-informed decisions about further education and training and employment opportunities; and

◇ Prepare students who may choose to enter the workforce directly after high school with levels of skill and knowledge in a particular career area that will be valued in the marketplace (executive summary, 1).

In addition, ACTE makes nine specific recommendations:

1. Establish a clear system goal of career and college readiness for all students.

2. Create a positive school culture that stresses personalization in planning and decision making.

3. Create a positive school culture that stresses personalization in relationships.

4. Dramatically improve how and where academic content is taught.

5. Create incentives for students to pursue the core curriculum in an interest-based context.

6. Support high-quality teaching in all content areas.

7. Offer flexible learning opportunities to encourage re-entry and completion.

8. Create system incentives and supports for connection of CTE and high school re-design efforts.

9. Move beyond "seat-time" and narrowly defined knowledge and skills.

Advocates for CTE have argued, successfully, that southern states that have reduced vocational education courses in high schools have seen a rise in high school dropouts. Likewise, CTE is strongly supported by the nation's governors, and it has major champions in the U.S. Congress. Advocates claim that CTE enhances students' academic achievement, at the same time preparing them for in-demand jobs, and providing business and industry with skilled workers needed to compete in the 21st-century economy and spur local economies. CTE leads to postsecondary learning opportunities and increased earning in the workplace (Driscoll 2005).

The Center for Evaluation and Education Policy (CEEP), in an article by Zapf, Spradlin, and Plucker titled "Redesigning High Schools to Prepare Students for the Future: 2006 Update," noted that

> student engagement in academic activities is … a crucial aspect of the learning process and is necessary to obtain the requisite knowledge, skills and abilities to be successful in subsequent educational and work-related endeavors…. Recent research indicates that many high school students are not engaged in academically related behaviors.

In another example,

> 50 percent of responding high school students (HSSSE—High School Survey of Student Engagement 2005) indicated they spent four hours or less *each week* preparing for class. Only four percent reported spending 20 or more hours per week preparing for class. Students enrolled in honors or college-prep courses reported spending twice as much time per week preparing for class than students in special education or career and vocational courses. (HSSSE 2005, 2)

> Forty-two percent of students reported that they had sometimes or never integrated information from a number of sources (e.g., books, interviews, Internet resources) for a paper or project. Similarly, only 32 percent of general education students indicated they regularly synthesized information from a variety of subjects. Comparatively, 46 percent of students in honors or college-prep programs reported doing so. Furthermore, only 57 percent of respondents indicated they participated regularly in class discussions. (HSSSE 2005)

CEEP notes further that the Bill and Melinda Gates Foundation has provided nearly $1 billion in grants (1994–2006) to high schools for specific reform projects including "Knowledge Is Power Schools" and "High Tech High Schools," as well as working with other organizations to create smaller, more personalized learning communities within large high schools. CEEP also points out the effectiveness of other high school reform models, notably "High Schools That Work"; "Talent Development High School"; "Career Academies"; and "First Things First" (CEEP, 6–7).

So what do school library media centers have to do with all of this redesigning and CTE planning? So far, not much that is visible. Why? As speculation, it seems likely that few school librarians have backgrounds in vocational education or career and technical education. We tend to have undergraduate degrees in education or English or history, and this would seem to indicate that we tend to use library media budgets to support areas of the high school curriculum to which we can more easily relate, the academic. We tend, in fact, to support the students and teachers and curricula of the college bound, with attention to the requirements of the special needs students. The "forgotten half" students, the general diploma students, the regular students, slip under our collective radar. Not deliberately, of course. We just don't see them. Yet, these are the students who may be most in need of our special skills and resources, most in need of abilities to determine when they have a need for information, the ability to be able to identify likely sources of information, locating those resources, selecting specific resources considered of most value, recording and arranging the information in a manner useful to their needs, analyzing and synthesizing the information, communicating what they have learned, and evaluating the result.

These forgotten students, the ones, by all reports, most likely of either dropping out of high school before graduation, or moving directly into the workforce rather than onto a college campus, are probably more difficult to reach. For the most part, school librarians do not appear to reach out to work with CTE instructors in our schools, nor do we have much knowledge of those specific curricula. And even though the CTE literature neither recognizes us nor our potential for these students and programs, it seems advisable to develop outreach agendas for those curricular areas and faculty.

The Southern Regional Education Board, through one of its services (EvaluTech—www.evalutech.sreb.org), has provided an excellent graphic illustration of the development of "21st Century Skills and Information and Communication Technologies Literacies" (www.evalutech.sreb.org/ 21stcentury/LiteracySkills.asp). In two formats, the organization has traced the development of information and communication technologies literacy through key documents, beginning with *A Nation at Risk* (1983) through *Route 21: An Interactive Guide to 21st Century Learning* (2004), with links to each publication. It includes "National Forum on Information Literacy" (American Library Association 1987) and "The Nine Information Literacy Standards for Student Learning" (American Association of School Librarians 1998), as well as specific references from "SCANS Report" (U.S. Department of Labor 1991), the American Association of School Administrators (AASA), U.S. Department of Education studies and documents, U.S. Department of Commerce, the International Society for Technology in Education (ISTE), and of course the Partnership for 21st Century Skills and the American Council on Education, Business and Higher Education, the Association of College and Research Libraries (ACRL 2003), and the Educational Testing Service (2001–2003).

References

American Association of School Librarians. "The Nine Information Literacy Standards for Student Learning." 1998. http://www.ala.org/ala/aasl/aaslproftools/ informationpower/informationliteracy.htm.

American Library Association. "National Forum on Information Literacy." 1987. http://www.infolit.org.

Association for Career and Technical Education. *Reinventing the American High School for the 21st Century: Strengthening a New Vision for the American High School through the Experiences and Resources of Career and Technical Education.* Alexandria, VA: Association for Career and Technical Education, 2006.

Blazek, Ronald D. "Teacher Utilization of Nonrequired Library Materials in Mathematics and the Effect on Pupil Use." PhD diss., University of Illinois at Urbana-Champaign, 1971.

Burks, Freda A. E. "Nature and Extent of School Library Use in Selected High Schools in the Greater Dallas-Fort Worth, Texas Area." PhD diss., Texas Woman's University, 1993.

CEEP (Center for Evaluation and Education Policy). 2004. http://www.indiana.edu/~ceep/.

Dorin, A. "Current Practices in Vocational High School Libraries in New York City." EdD diss., New York University, 1960.

Driscoll, Christine M. "ACTE 'Capitol View.'" March 2005. Available from http://www.acteonline.org (accessed April 18, 2007).

Ducat, M. "Student and Faculty Use of the Library in Three Secondary Schools." DLS diss., Columbia University, 1960.

Hartley, N. "Faculty Utilization of the High School Library." PhD diss., Peabody College for Teachers of Vanderbilt University, 1980.

Indiana University. *High School Survey of Student Engagement 2005: What We Can Learn from High School Students.* Bloomington: Indiana University, 2005.

Manikas, J. "The Shop Collection in Vocational-Technical Programs: A Perceptual Study of Two-Year Faculty and Librarians." PhD diss., The Florida State University, 1981.

National Commission on Teaching & America's Future (U.S.). *What Matters Most: Teaching for America's Future: Report of the National Commission on Teaching & America's Future*, 1st ed. New York: National Commission on Teaching & America's Future, 1996.

North Carolina State Department of Public Instruction. "Advisory List of Instructional Media for Vocational Education." Raleigh, NC: North Carolina State Department of Public Instruction, 1977–1978.

Parrott, Marietta, Marilena Borgna, and Barbara Keeline. *Vocational Students' and Instructors' Perceptions and Usage of COS Library Services.* Springfield, VA: ERIC Document Reproduction Service, 1982.

Partnership for 21st Century Skills. "Route 21: An Interactive Guide to 21st Century Learning." 2004. http://www.21stcenturyskills.org/Route21/GuideTOC.asp.

Peifly, Maryann C. "A Time Series Study of Selected Variables in the Delivery of Vocational Education in New Jersey, 1974–1979." EdD thesis, Rutgers University, 1981.

School Libraries Work! Scholastic Library Publishing. 2006. http://www.scholastic. com/librarians/printables/downloads/slw%5F2006.pdf (accessed 18 April 2007).

Southern Regional Education Board. "EvaluTech." http://www.evalutech.sreb.org (accessed 18 April 2007).

———. "21st Century Skills: From *A Nation at Risk* to ICT Literacy." http:// www.evalutech.sreb.org/21stcentury/Literacyskills.asp.

Thomas, Margie J. K. "School Library Media Services and the Integration of the Vocational Education and Academic Curricula in Three Florida High Schools: A Comparative Case Study." PhD diss., The Florida State University, 2000.

United States Department of Education. *A Nation at Risk: The Imperative for Educational Reform: A Report to the Nation and the Secretary of Education, United States Department of Education.* 1983. http://purl.access.gpo.gov/ GPO/LPS3244.

Zapf, Jason S., Terry E. Spradlin, and Jonathan A. Plucker. "Redesigning High Schools to Prepare Students for the Future: 2006 Update." *Education Policy Brief* 4, no. 6 (2006).

4
Exploring the Information Needs of the School-to-Work Student

"In the end we retain from our studies only that which we practically apply."

Johann Wolfgang von Goethe

"The mission of the school library media center is to ensure that students and staff are effective users of ideas and information."

Information Power, 9

Every school librarian in the nation should be excited and challenged by the high school reform or high school re-design movement and initiatives. For those not already involved and engaged in planning for some curricular and organizational changes and implementation at the school level, the time to begin is now. Changes in curriculum and organization at the school level provide the opportunity for the school librarian to examine or re-examine the library collection and programs, and to advocate for funding to better meet the needs of all students, faculty, and programs that are receiving school and community attention.

As a first step, school librarians should examine the "Comprehensive School Reform Program" at the U.S. Department of Education website (www.ed.gov/programs/compreform/index.html). Note that funding for school reform has been available from the U.S. Department of Education to individual state departments of education to assist in bringing about planning for positive changes in high school curricula and programs, and those states that develop plans for high school reform can be eligible for federal money. An examination of state department of education websites reveals that many, and probably most states, have such plans, or are in the process of developing models for examining high schools and high school programs in their states.

Refer also to the Partnership for 21st Century Skills (www.21stcenturyskills.org) site for "Results that Matter: 21st Century Skills and High School Reform" (www.21stcenturyskills.org/index.php?option=com_content& task=view&id=204&Ite). A good deal of U.S. Department of Education, as well as state departments of education, funding is tied to student success on the various high-stakes testing initiatives mandated by most states. This should be an encouragement to school librarians, since we know that our programs, resources, and services play a pivotal role in student academic achievement.

The next investigatory step is to determine the form high school redesign is taking in your state, in your district, and in your school. Do proposed changes appear to emphasize the Career Academy model? High Schools That Work? KIPP Schools? High Tech High Schools? Tech Prep programs? Academic magnet schools? IB programs? Chapter 2 provides brief descriptions of some of these programs, models, and designs.

As the Cheshire Cat told Alice (*Alice in Wonderland*), in response to her request for direction, if she didn't know or care where she wanted to go, "then it doesn't matter which way you go." School librarians should have a good grip on the direction that their school, community, district, and state are going in order to evaluate the role of the school library in that or those settings.

The next step is to ensure an understanding of school demographics. It is not only possible but fairly easy to get such a picture for almost every school in the country. If the school itself does not publish composite demographics, test scores, and graduation rates on its website, that information is very likely available through the principal or counseling office. The district offices are another good source of basic data, as is the state department of education. Some school and/or district education websites call particular attention to special programs in place, for example, an arts magnet program, an information technology career academy, or a health care career track.

Each public school in the country is required to make available, on a yearly basis, a certain amount of composite information about its students, faculty, curriculum, mandated test results, number of students taking Advanced Placement and honors classes (and how they did in those classes), the number of students qualified for free or reduced lunches, students requiring special assistance (special education), and breakdowns by gender, race, and ethnicity. These reports are supposed to be available to all, either through the school itself, the district, the state department of education, or the U.S. Department of Education, National Center for Education Statistics.

For instance, Central Noble High School in Albion, Indiana, in the 2006–2007 school year had an enrollment of 453 students in grades 9 to 12, according to the Indiana Department of Education (http://mustang. doe.state.in.us/SEARCH/snapshot.cfm?schl=6453).

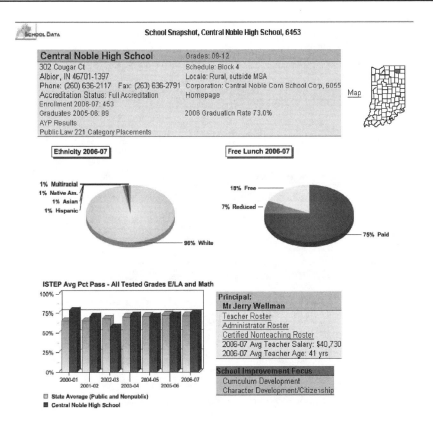

School Snapshot, Central Noble High School, 6453

The school is classified as rural, outside MSA (Municipal Service Area), and operates on a Block 4 schedule. The pupil/teacher ratio is 16 to 1. Ninety-six percent of the students are white, with about 1 percent each classified as multiracial, Native American, Asian, or Hispanic. Eighteen percent of the student body receives a free lunch, another 7 percent a reduced lunch price. Eighty-nine students graduated in the spring of 2006 (73.0 percent graduation rate). For the class of 2005, the Indiana Department of Education reported that of the 406 students that year, 225 were male, 181 female. Thirty-four of the 82 Central Noble graduates of 2005 were attending a four-year college, six were attending a two-year college, nine were at vocational or technical schools, one was in the military, and 32 were not pursuing education beyond high school. Similar information can be located through the National Center for Education Statistics (http://nces.ed.gov/ccd/schoolsearch/).

The U.S. Census Bureau (factfinder.census.gov) for the 2000 census year in Noble County, Indiana, tells us that the total population for the county was 46,275, of which 50.4 percent were male and 49.6 percent female, with a median age of 33.3 years (this must not include my aunt, who is 85!). Ninety-four percent of the population is white, 7 percent Hispanic/Latino, 4 percent Native Hawaiian/Pacific Islander, and less than 1 percent each Black/African American, American Indian/Alaska Native, or

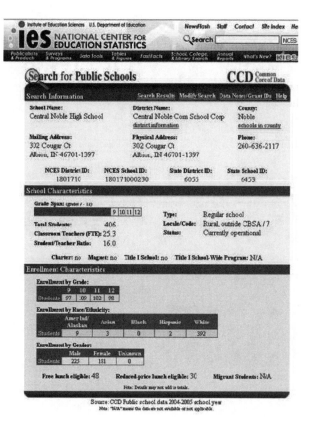

Source: CCD Public school data 2004–2005 school year
Note: "N/A" means the data are not available or not applicable.

Asian. (I know that this does not add to 100 percent, but that is what the bureau says!) Seventy-seven percent reported being a high school graduate, and about 11 percent reported having a college degree. At least demographically, the students at Central Noble High School appear to reflect the population of the county as a whole.

Of course, this data does not address the personalities, hopes, and dreams of those students. It mentions nothing of the beautiful singing voice, the potential astronaut, the talented athlete, the math genius, the natural-born mechanic, the science buff, or the romantic young couple who have plans to marry and then begin their own small business operation. That's where collaborating with classroom teachers and administrators and working with the students comes in. Particularly in a smaller school, it is possible to identify the personalities and the hopes and dreams and "market" the library media center materials, program, and services to individuals, curricular areas, and student activities and programs within that building. This can be most effective by talking to the students and teachers, asking questions, soliciting student and faculty input for collection development or programming, planning outreach programs, and making an effort to involve each student in library media center activities as appropriate.

In a larger school, for instance, Boone High School in Orlando, Florida (the author's alma mater), there were in the 2004–2005 school year

General Characteristics - show more >>	Number	Percent	U.S.
Total population	46,275		
Male	23,310	50.4	49.1%
Female	22,965	49.6	50.9%
Median age (years)	33.3	(X)	35.3
Under 5 years	3,695	8.0	6.8%
18 years and over	32,851	71.0	74.3%
65 years and over	5,102	11.0	12.4%
One race	45,841	99.1	97.6%
White	43,490	94.0	75.1%
Black or African American	189	0.4	12.3%
American Indian and Alaska Native	115	0.2	0.9%
Asian	168	0.4	3.6%
Native Hawaiian and Other Pacific Islander	9	0.0	0.1%
Some other race	1,870	4.0	5.5%
Two or more races	434	0.9	2.4%
Hispanic or Latino (of any race)	3,299	7.1	12.5%
Household population	45,613	98.6	97.2%
Group quarters population	662	1.4	2.8%
Average household size	2.73	(X)	2.59
Average family size	3.19	(X)	3.14
Total housing units	18,233		
Occupied housing units	16,696	91.6	91.0%
Owner-occupied housing units	13,022	78.0	66.2%
Renter-occupied housing units	3,674	22.0	33.8%
Vacant housing units	1,537	8.4	9.0%

Social Characteristics - show more >>	Number	Percent	U.S.
Population 25 years and over	28,554		
High school graduate or higher	22,088	77.3	80.4%
Bachelor's degree or higher	3,164	11.1	24.4%
Civilian veterans (civilian population 18 years and over)	3,968	12.1	12.7%
Disability status (population 5 years and over)	7,266	17.3	19.3%
Foreign born	2,260	4.9	11.1%
Male, Now married, except separated (population 15 years and over)	10,821	61.5	56.7%
Female, Now married, except separated (population 15 years and over)	10,600	60.4	52.1%
Speak a language other than English at home (population 5 years and over)	4,092	9.8	17.9%

FACT SHEET

United States | Indiana | **Noble County**
Noble County, Indiana

Economic Characteristics - show more >>	Number	Percent	U.S.
In labor force (population 16 years and over)	23,803	69.4	63.9%
Mean travel time to work in minutes (workers 16 years and over)	21.2	(X)	25.5
Median household income in 1999 (dollars)	42,700	(X)	41,994
Median family income in 1999 (dollars)	49,037	(X)	50,046
Per capita income in 1999 (dollars)	17,896	(X)	21,587
Families below poverty level	688	5.8	9.2%

Housing Characteristics - show more >>	Number	Percent	U.S.
Single-family owner-occupied homes	9,365		
Median value (dollars)	88,600	(X)	119,600
Median of selected monthly owner costs	(X)	(X)	
With a mortgage (dollars)	794	(X)	1,088
Not mortgaged (dollars)	237	(X)	295
(X) Not applicable.			
Source: U.S. Census Bureau, Summary File 1 (SF 1) and Summary File 3 (SF 3)			

3,346 students in grades 8 through 12. Boone is classed by the National Center for Educational Statistics (NCES; http://nces.ed.gov/ccd/school search) as a regular school, in a mid/central city location. The pupil teacher ration is 20.2 to 1. Of the students, 1,656 were male, 1,690 female. Eight students were American Indian/Alaska Native, 59 Asian, 479 Black, 672 Hispanic, and 2,128 White. Eight hundred thirty-eight of the students were eligible for free lunch, another 203 for reduced price lunch (31 percent total), and there were three migrant students.

The reported graduation rate for Boone students in 2004–2005 was 91.2 percent. The Florida Department of Education's "School Report Card" gave Boone a grade of B for the 2005–2006 academic year. Comments on the state department of education website access (http://schoolgrades.fldoe.org) were that "Black, Hispanic, economically disadvantaged, limited English proficiency, students with disabilities students in this school need improvement in Reading.... Limited English proficiency, students with disabilities students in this school need improvement in Math."

The 2005 American Community Survey for Orange County, Florida (U.S. Census Bureau, http://factfinder.census.gov), indicated that county population was 1,002,849, 49.5 percent of them male, and 50.5 percent female. The population identified itself as being 64.2 percent white, 19.8 percent black or African American, 23.5 percent Hispanic or Latino, 4.4 percent Asian (yes, that is 111 percent, but that's what the table says). Over 85 percent reported having a high school diploma, and about 27 percent reported a bachelor's degree or higher. Some 70.4 percent were in the labor force.

Employment prospects for local areas can also be accessed through the U.S. Census Bureau (http://factfinder.census.gov) to the extent that they reveal the number of establishments at the local level involved in manufacturing; retail trade; information; real estate and rental and leasing; professional, scientific, and technical services; administrative and

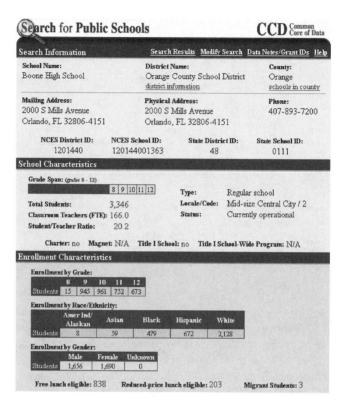

support and waste administration and remediation service; educational services; health care and social assistance; arts, entertainment, and recreation; accommodation and food services; and the wonderfully generic "other." More specific demographic and employment information will, of course, be available through state and local departments of labor, agriculture, education, and so forth.

The movement for high school reform is real, and school librarians should view these changes with enthusiasm because of the opportunity for increased visibility for the library media center and its materials, resources, services, and programs. That, of course, requires that high school librarians examine the type or model of reform that is coming about in their school or district. Each state and school district will look different from its neighbors, so examine the state department of education website in your state to see what changes are coming about.

Indiana had a Rationale for Redesign, according to their website (www.doe.state.in.us/highschoolredesign):

◇ Delivery of instruction and curriculum lack the relevance needed for today's students. More of a focus on the use of technology and online learning should exist in all high schools.

◇ Structures that are called schools are outdated and function under the factory model that was developed in the 1950s.

General Characteristics - show more >>	Estimate	Percent	U.S.	Margin of Error
Total population	1,002,849			*****
Male	496,427	49.5	49.0%	+/-326
Female	506,422	50.5	51.0%	+/-326
Median age (years)	34.3	(X)	36.4	+/-0.2
Under 5 years	78,471	7.8	7.0%	+/-215
18 years and over	737,852	73.6	74.6%	*****
65 years and over	92,532	9.2	12.1%	+/-308
One race	981,560	97.9	98.1%	+/-3,199
White	644,294	64.2	74.7%	+/-9,975
Black or African American	198,313	19.8	12.1%	+/-2,692
American Indian and Alaska Native	4,074	0.4	0.8%	+/-1,508
Asian	44,172	4.4	4.3%	+/-1,448
Native Hawaiian and Other Pacific Islander	39	0.0	0.1%	+/-62
Some other race	90,668	9.0	6.0%	+/-10,872
Two or more races	21,289	2.1	1.9%	+/-3,199
Hispanic or Latino (of any race)	235,871	23.5	14.5%	*****
Household population	1,002,849			*****
Group quarters population	(X)	(X)	(X)	(X)
Average household size	2.56	(X)	2.60	+/-0.02
Average family size	3.15	(X)	3.18	+/-0.05
Total housing units	423,688			*****
Occupied housing units	391,440	92.4	89.2	+/-3,393
Owner-occupied housing units	232,093	59.3	66.9	+/-5,432
Renter-occupied housing units	159,347	40.7	33.1	+/-5,855
Vacant housing units	32,248	7.6	10.8	+/-3,393

Social Characteristics - show more >>	Estimate	Percent	U.S.	Margin of Error
Population 25 years and over	641,574			+/-279
High school graduate or higher	(X)	85.8	84.2%	(X)
Bachelor's degree or higher	(X)	27.3	27.2%	(X)
Civilian veterans (civilian population 18 years and over)	70,322	9.5	10.9%	+/-3,495
Disability status (population 5 years and over)	106,771	11.6	14.9%	+/-5,566
Foreign born	184,026	19.4	12.4%	+/-10,479
Male, Now married, except separated (population 15 years and over)	200,455	52.3	55.9%	+/-5,767
Female, Now married, except separated (population 15 years and over)	187,021	47.0	51.0%	+/-5,842
Speak a language other than English at home (population 5 years and over)	275,878	29.8	19.4%	+/-10,311

Economic Characteristics - show more >>	Estimate	Percent	U.S.	Margin of Error
In labor force (population 16 years and over)	540,087	70.4	65.9%	+/-6,555
Mean travel time to work in minutes (workers 16 years and over)	25.8	(X)	25.1	+/-0.5
Median household income (in 2005 inflation-adjusted dollars)	44,236	(X)	46,242	+/-1,691
Median family income (in 2005 inflation-adjusted dollars)	51,877	(X)	55,832	+/-2,097
Per capita income (in 2005 inflation-adjusted dollars)	23,805	(X)	25,035	+/-824
Families below poverty level	(X)	9.2	10.2	(X)
Individuals below poverty level	(X)	12.6	13.3	(X)

Housing Characteristics - show more >>	Estimate	Percent	U.S.	Margin of Error
Owner-occupied homes	232,093			+/-5,432
Median value (dollars)	201,900	(X)	167,500	+/-5,328
Median of selected monthly owner costs				
With a mortgage (dollars)	1,296	(X)	1,295	+/-29
Not mortgaged (dollars)	381	(X)	369	+/-13

FACT SHEET

United States | Florida | Orange County
Orange County, Florida

❖ Accountability is limited to data collections from testing and serves as a punitive incentive for improvement. Accountability needs to reach into every classroom of every content area.

Along with the Vision (www.doe.in.gov/HighSchoolredesign/welcome.HTML), the Indiana DOE suggests a number of re-design model sites and high school models, to assist local communities.

In Florida (www.fldoe.org/hsreform/strategies.asp) the state department of education identified three goals for high school reform:

❖ Increase the academic achievement levels of high school students (i.e., Increase the percent of graduates prepared to enter postsecondary institutions without remediation).

❖ Increase the percent of high school graduates.

❖ Increase the percent of graduates who begin their postsecondary path to college or career while in a Florida high school.

This document/plan was expanded to include specific strategies for implementing these broad goals, including offering differentiated diplomas based on a student's academic path, instituting smaller learning communities, implementing incentives and disincentives for student achievement and high school graduation, and providing a wider range of choices and alternatives, including career academies, schools within schools, virtual schools, among others.

Neither Florida nor Indiana so much as hint at the place or role of the library media center within these re-design plans, though Florida suggests that schools "organize Book Fairs to get parents involved" in increasing literacy. Other states, of course, may be more aware of the role and value of library media programs and might include specific references to them.

The Role of the School Librarian in High School Reform and Information Literacy Integration

Any change in school curriculum, graduation requirements, differentiated diplomas (graduation tracks), must be addressed by the school librarian with plans to meet these identified student/curriculum needs. For instance, a number of states look to the idea of "career academies" within high schools to involve students in hands-on learning focused on a particular career area, basing this specialized instruction on strong academic underpinnings. While career focus areas or clusters will vary from one area of the country to another, they will generally try to reflect post–high school educational opportunities in the area, as well as local area employment possibilities and employer needs. So one might see agriscience and biotechnology; business and marketing; communication and the arts; engineering and manufacturing; health and human services; hospitality and tourism (these from Florida); or very specific programs (criminal justice, law, and finance; horticultural, environmental, and marine science; digital media and marketing; sports science; automotive service technology).

California's Career Technical Education (CCTE) model curriculum standards (re-vamped in 2005; www.cde.ca.gov/re/pn/fd/documents/career-techstnd.pdf) are organized in 15 industry sectors or groupings of interrelated occupations and broad industries. Each sector has two or more career pathways, California's "Industry Sectors":

- ✧ Agriculture and Natural Resources
- ✧ Arts, Media, and Entertainment
- ✧ Building Trades and Construction
- ✧ Education, Child Development, and Family Services
- ✧ Energy and Utilities
- ✧ Engineering and Design
- ✧ Fashion and Interior Design
- ✧ Finance and Business
- ✧ Health Science and Medical Technology
- ✧ Hospitality, Tourism, and Recreation
- ✧ Information Technology
- ✧ Manufacturing and Product Development
- ✧ Marketing, Sales, and Service
- ✧ Public Services
- ✧ Transportation

It is not, of course, necessary or even recommended, and probably not possible, that all high schools in California offer all of these career track options. Choices would depend upon local communities, local employment opportunities, and student options for post secondary education.

In the models and programs examined in chapter 2, the career tracks are designed in such a way that each student in a career focus program meets district and state graduation requirements by completing mathematics, English/language arts, social studies, and science requirements for graduation, and then, sometimes as early as the ninth grade (freshman year), uses "electives" toward a general career area. A health care track freshman course schedule might therefore include English/language arts, mathematics, science (biology, perhaps), social studies, and electives such as "Health Care Careers," "Technologies in Health Care," "Food Preparation for Institutions," or another elective in music or art or foreign language.

Some high schools have established admission requirements for at least a portion of their career track programs. For instance, if high school students in "Information Technology" routinely participated in paid (or unpaid) internships, in "tech prep" opportunities that lead to advanced technical training beyond high school, and/or in good entry-level jobs upon graduating from high school, the reputation of that track/curriculum and the instructors in that program would cause students to line up for a seat in those classrooms. In cases such as these, programs may require students to have a specific grade point average (GPA), perhaps 2.5 or higher, in previous coursework; to have good attendance and discipline records; and to obtain faculty recommendations.

As stated previously, students in career/tech programs will, of course, meet school and state graduation requirements (probably about 20 to 24 credits, usually including four years of English/language arts; two to three years of mathematics; two to three years of science; and two to three years of social studies, to include history, government, geography, economics; and electives, which in this instance would be course concentrations in the career/tech area).

For the school librarian involved in high school reform, as all should be, with the possibilities of revamped curriculum and more stringent academic requirements for all students, the first step is to examine the requirements of the existing and new programs being offered. To support a program in information technology, for instance, one would need new and current print and non-print resources on digital media, digital recording for radio and television, electronic publishing, networking and telecommunications, web design and web management, among others. Hospitality and tourism would certainly require print and non-print material in communication skills and business skills, layered upon English/language arts, mathematics, science, social sciences, and, of course, the ability to use technologies in various degrees. Agribusiness? C'mon, science, science, and more science, along with business, technology, and math. And if your students intend to market their agri-products, they will need English/language arts, communication, social studies (knowledge of global business economies), and some knowledge of the business and marketing world.

Getting to know the new curriculum and course requirements presents a wonderful opportunity for outreach and marketing, and a beginning to working collaboratively with the CTE instructors in order to introduce information literacy and technology skills into each class and each area.

So many good titles are available on collaboration and collection development designed to build information literacy skills that making only a few recommendations is difficult. The experienced school library media specialist will have a number of titles on hand, which might include:

Burkhardt, J. M., M. C. MacDonald, and A. J. Rathemacher. *Teaching Information Literacy: 35 Practical Standards-Based Exercises for College Students*. ALA, 2003.

Ely, D. P., and T. Plomp. *Classic Writings on Instructional Technology*. Libraries Unlimited, 1996.

Koechlin, C., and S. Zwaan. *Build Your Own Information Literate School*. Hi Willow, 2004.

Morris, B. J. *Administering the School Library Media Center*, 4th ed. Libraries Unlimited, 2004.

Stanley, D. B. *Practical Steps to the Research Process for High School*. Libraries Unlimited, 1999.

Whitley, P., C. Olson, and S. Goodwin. *99 Jumpstarts to Research: Topic Guides for Finding Information on Current Issues*. Libraries Unlimited, 2001.

Woolls, B. *The School Library Media Manager*, 4th ed. Libraries Unlimited, 2008.

Zweizig, D. L., and D. M. Hopkins. *Lessons from Library Power: Enriching Teaching and Learning*. Libraries Unlimited, 1999.

It is of major importance, particularly in working with a part of the faculty with whom one may not have worked previously, to make the time to find out about each specific course being taught, what the course requirements are, textbooks (if any), pertinent websites or databases, suggested or recommended reading or viewing lists, course projects, testing and evaluation, and so forth. Once the school librarian has a good picture of course and curriculum objectives, it is advisable to begin working collaboratively with the classroom CTE teacher to identify good sources of information for any specific topic, and to teach students how to access and use that information. Whitely, Olson, and Goodwin (above) provide some excellent guides and resources for pinpointing information sources and search terms on a variety of current information issues. If your school has a focus on health care, for instance, your students will need access to information resources on abortion, alcohol advertising, alternative medicine, animal research, assisted suicide, athletes as role models, attention deficit hyperactivity disorder, child care, cloning and genetic research, drug testing, eating disorders, FDA and medicine approval, fitness for children, health insurance, hunger in America, sports and lifelong benefits, and tobacco (Whitely, Olson, and Goodwin 2001, v–vii), among others.

The next step is to analyze the current print and non-print collections in the library media center. Some commercial library automation programs now include a report module that will allow you to do this fairly quickly and easily. Reports generated can include the composite age of the collection, as well as the age of various collection components (e.g., the 500s). See an excellent article by Amy Hart in the February 2003 *Library Media Connection* titled "Collection Analysis: Powerful Ways to Collect, Analyze, and Present Your Data" (36–39). This particular article provides a wonderful step-by-step guide to using the Follett Library Resources product. The BroDart Corporation likewise works with school librarians to do collection analysis, as does OCLC's WorldCat, though it focuses on public and academic libraries. Baker & Taylor is also able to provide this service. Check with your library automation service provider to see if the company includes a report module that can be used for collection analysis. Excellent print guides to non-electronic collection analysis have been done by Carol Doll and Pamela Barron (2002) and Nancy Everhart (chapter 3 of *Evaluating the School Library Media Center: Analysis Techniques and Research Practices*, 1998).

If using an online library automation program, the reports generated will enable you to look at specific areas of the collection necessary to support career or school-to-work agendas. For instance, a program in information technology would mandate some specific collection development effort in the Dewey 000s (Computers and Computer Science), the 300s (Social Sciences—Law, Public Administration, Commerce, and Communication), and certainly the 600s (Applied Technology). Materials here must be kept current—in most instances, five years is too old, unless your students spend time with the history of computers and technology. Be prepared to develop lists of pertinent websites and, certainly, access to non-print material such as DVDs.

In order to support curriculum that focuses on school-to-work students (our forgotten half), we in school libraries need to look at both print and non-print material and access to information in all formats that support a more "hands-on" curriculum while continuing to support our more traditional base, the so-called academic curriculum. In doing so, it is wise to remember not to purchase support materials with titles such as *Auto Mechanics for the Functionally Illiterate* (I made this up, folks; it is *not* real!). High school sophomores and juniors and seniors may well have had academic difficulties in the past, but that does not mean that they are dumb or illiterate.

Many of these new materials that you consider should be non-fiction. Fortunately, there are a number of good general guides to identify newer materials in the 000–900 schema. Refer to Wilson's *High School Library Catalog*; *University Press Books: Selected for Public and Secondary School Libraries* (selected by a committee of Librarians from the American Association of School Librarians and the Small and Medium Sized Library Committee of the Public Library Association); or *More Outstanding Books for the College Bound* (Young Adult Library Services Association). For heaven's sake, make use of the recommended titles from the American Library

Association, the American Association of School Librarians, and the Young Adult Library Services Association.

But don't forget the fun stuff. High school age people will read and access and use information about topics of interest. "Fun" books in science and technology might include Kendall Haven's *100 Greatest Science Inventions of All Time* (2006), which includes a chapter on the zipper and Velcro, the ballpoint pen, and the communications satellite, among others. Haven provides both historical and technological perspectives. University Press Books (noted above and available online at www.aaupnet.org/librarybooks) includes such titles as *Native Trees of the Midwest: Identification, Wildlife Values and Landscaping Use* by Sally S. and Harmon Weeks and George Parker (2005), among other suggestions.

More fun stuff? Sports, music, cars, motorcycles, more music, more sports, personal grooming and dress, poetry, more music, and more sports. Remember that many students without college ambitions are active athletes, musicians, and artists. And joke books. And don't forget the popular magazines. High school young people, regardless of their future education or careers, will use your school library if you make it a place that is welcoming, and that has information and materials of immediate interest to them, that they can enjoy, and ultimately that they can use.

Don't forget the fiction. Realistic fiction, of course, but fantasy and science fiction, mysteries, humor, historical fiction, romance, graphic novels, and manga and anime. "If you build it, they will come" (from *Field of Dreams*, the motion picture). Who's to say that we all don't learn as much from the novels we read, or fun non-fiction, than from the rather dry textbooks that persist in our classrooms. Granted, the "fun stuff" won't prep kids for the state-mandated testing, but they will be reading, and becoming increasingly literate, as well as becoming increasingly adept at locating information dealing with classroom and curricular topics assigned to them.

References

American Association of School Librarians and Association for Educational Communications and Technology. *Information Power: Building Partnerships for Learning*. Chicago: American Library Association. 1998.

Association of American University Presses. *University Press Books: Selected for Public and Secondary School Libraries*. 2006. http://www.aaupnet.org/librarybooks/.

California Department of Education. "California Career Technical Education Model Curriculum Standards." 2006. http://www.cde.ca.gov/re/pn/fd/documents/careertechstnd.pdf.

Carroll, Lewis [pseud. of Charles Lutwidge Dodgson]. *Alice's Adventures in Wonderland*. 1865.

Doll, Carol, and Pamela Barron. *Managing and Analyzing Your Collection: A Practical Guide for Small Libraries and School Media Centers*. Chicago: American Library Association, 2002.

Everhart, Nancy. *Evaluating the School Library Media Center: Analysis Techniques and Research Practices*. Englewood, CO: Libraries Unlimitied, 1998.

Florida Department of Education. "Florida School Grades." 2005. http://school grades.fldoe.org/.

———. "High School Reform." 2005. http://www.fldoe.org/hsreform/strategies.asp.

Hart, Amy. "Collection Analysis: Powerful Ways to Collect, Analyze, and Present You Data." *Library Media Connection* 21, no. 5 (2003): 36–39.

Haven, Kendall. *100 Greatest Science Inventions of All Time*. Westport, CT: Libraries Unlimited, 2006.

High School Library Catalog. New York: H.W. Wilson.

Indiana Department of Education. "High School Redesign." 2007. http://www.doe. state.in.us/highschoolredesign. http://www.doe.in.gov/highschoolredesign/ pdf/roundtable_publication.pdf.

———. "School Snapshot of Central Noble High School." 2007. http:// mustang.doe.state.in.us/SEARCH/snapshot.cfm?schl=6453.

National Center for Education Statistics. "Search for Public Schools." http://nces. ed.gov/ccd/schoolsearch.

Partnership for 21st Century Skills. 2004. http://www.21stcenturyskills.org.

Robinson, Phil Alden. *Field of Dreams*. 1989.

U.S. Census Bureau. "Fact Finder." 2000. http://factfinder.census.gov.

U.S. Department of Education. "Comprehensive School Reform Program." http:// www.ed.gov/programs/compreform/index.html.

Weeks, Sally S., and Harmon Weeks, and George Parker. *Native Trees of the Midwest: Identification, Wildlife Values and Landscaping Use*. West Lafayette, IN: Purdue University Press, 2005.

5
Information and Technology Literacy Applied

"Tell me and I forget. Teach me and I remember. Involve me and I learn."

Benjamin Franklin

Virtually every plan, model, or idea for reforming or redefining or remaking the American high school stresses the need for all students to be information and technologically literate. *Information Power: Building Partnerships for Learning* (ALA 1998) with its "Nine Information Literacy Standards for Student Learning" is among the documents referred to by Southern Region Education Board's EvaluTech in "21st Century Skills and Information and Communications Technologies Literacy: From *A Nation at Risk* to ICT Literacy" as being one of the "key literacy documents" (www.evalutech.sreb.org/21stcentury/LiteracySkills.asp).

The Partnership for 21st Century Skills (www.21stcenturyskills.org)—of which the American Association of School Librarians (AASL) is a member, along with the National Education Association, Dell, Apple, and other prestigious professional and corporate entities—has published a number of valuable reports that speak to the need for increased visibility and participation of the school librarian in today's educational systems. "Results that Matter: 21st Century Skills and High School Reform" (www.21stcentury skills.org/index.php?option=com_content&task=view&id=204&Ite) specifies a framework for addressing these needs comprised of the following components as noted previously in chapter 2 (14–15):

The former includes:

1. **Core Subject**
2. **21st-Century Content** to include:
   ✧ Global awareness
   ✧ Financial, economic, business, and entrepreneurial literacy
   ✧ Civic literacy
   ✧ Health and wellness awareness
3. **Learning and Thinking Skills** to include:
   ✧ Critical thinking and problem-solving skills
   ✧ Communication skills
   ✧ Creativity and innovation skills
   ✧ Collaboration skills
   ✧ Information and media literacy skills
   ✧ Contextual learning skills
4. **ICT Literacy**: Information and communications technology.
5. **Life Skills**, including:
   ✧ Leadership
   ✧ Ethics
   ✧ Accountability
   ✧ Adaptability
   ✧ Personal productivity
   ✧ Personal responsibility
   ✧ People skills
   ✧ Self-direction
   ✧ Social responsibility
6. **21st-Century Assessments**:

"Results that Matter" specifies that these 21st-century skills should be integrated with core academic subjects. *Are They Really Ready to Work?*, another report available from the Partnership for 21st Century Skills (http://www.21stcenturyskills.org/documents/FINAL_REPORT_PDF09-29-06.pdf) indicates that prospective employers cite the following as the most important skills:

✧ Professionalism/Work Ethic
✧ Oral and Written Communications
✧ Teamwork/Collaboration
✧ Critical Thinking/Problem Solving

"In fact, the findings indicate that applied skills on all educational levels trump basic knowledge and skills such as reading comprehension and mathematics" (Executive Summary, 9). The report lists applied skills as being:

✧ Critical Thinking/Problem Solving

✧ Oral Communications

✧ Written Communications

✧ Teamwork/Collaboration

✧ Diversity

✧ Information Technology Application

✧ Leadership

✧ Creativity/Innovation

✧ Lifelong Learning/Self-Direction

✧ Professionalism/Work Ethic

✧ Ethics/Social Responsibility

As information professionals, we know the importance of being "guides by the side" rather than "sages on stages," of being coaches rather than lecturers. Our professional literature frequently refers to the necessity of working with both students and teachers to help them to integrate the use of a variety of technologies to access and process information into academic content areas, as well as areas of personal interest. That should include the CTE programs in our high schools, and the "regular" English or science or math or social studies or physical education classes.

Information processing models such as Eisenberg and Berkowitz's Big 6 or those identified in *Information Power* apply equally to the student required to do a report on a disease caused by a virus, or looking for information on careers in sports medicine, or shopping for that first car, or training a young quarter horse. The process(es) as applied in individual schools varies in complexity, but generally follow(s) the pattern as defined by the Big 6 or AASL (above). The National Forum on Information Literacy (NFIL; www.infolit.org, 2006) defines Information Literacy as " ... the ability to know when there is a need for information, to be able to identify, locate, evaluate, and effectively use that information for the issue or problem at hand." The Forum, sponsored by the Syracuse Literacy Group, identifies other definitions related to Information Literacy:

Definitions Related to Information Literacy:

Business Literacy: The ability to use financial and business information to understand and make decisions that help an organization achieve success.

Computer Literacy: The ability to use a computer and its software to accomplish practical tasks.

(Continued)

Health Literacy: The degree to which individuals have the capacity to obtain, process, and understand basic health information and services needed to make appropriate health decisions.

Information Literacy: The ability to know when there is a need for information, to be able to identify, locate, evaluate, and effectively use that information for the issue or problem at hand.

Media Literacy: The ability to decode, analyze, evaluate, and produce communication in a variety of forms.

Technology Literacy: The ability to use media such as the Internet to effectively access and communicate information.

Visual Literacy: The ability, through knowledge of the basic visual elements, to understand the meaning and components of the image.

For additional terms and definitions, visit Definitions of Information Literacy and Related Terms from the University of South Florida (August 2003).

In addition, NFIL notes "Information Literacy Standards and Competencies," citing the AASL/Association for Educational Communications and Technology *Information Power*'s Nine Information Literacy Standards for Student Learning. They also cited "Information Literacy Competency Standards for Higher Education" from another division of the American Library Association, the Association of College and Research Libraries (ACRL). NFIL also provides a good bibliography of resources on information literacy, including some already noted in this work, at www.infolit.org/resources.html.

Developing information literacy and technology skills in all of our students is the area in which school librarians should excel as teachers. Research and writing over the past 100 years reminds us that, as Kenneth Eble, in *The Craft of Teaching* (1976) states:

> [College] professors gravitate to the bright, well-prepared students. They are easier to teach, and they appear to profit most from instruction, which may simply mean they are most like the professors. But in the increasing pluralism and decreasing professionalism of colleges and universities in the next decades, the master teacher is likely to be the one who can provide context for many kinds of students.

Our task, as school librarians, is to reach all of our students, recognizing the myriad learning styles and preferences and the increasingly demanding subject knowledge that they are expected to master to earn a high school diploma. In other words, we need to teach information access and evaluation *in context* with the curriculum or subject content.

Employing the "guide by the side" methodology and philosophy, the concept of integrating information literacy skills into areas of the curriculum in which we have not previously worked is still a fairly simple process that relies upon developing a good working relationship with the classroom teacher in order to understand individual course content and expectations for students. As Benjamin Franklin and Confucius wrote (not together, of course!), "Tell me and I forget. Teach me and I remember. Involve me and I learn."

Before students arrive in the library media center, the school librarian must know the class assignment and must have identified specific print and non-print material in or accessible through the media center. Perhaps students are coming to locate information about state representatives to the U.S. Congress and are required to document their resources. Information needed for the assignment might include the representative or senator's date and place of birth, marital status and children, educational background, religious affiliation, political party, congressional district represented, honors and awards, congressional committees, membership in professional or social organizations, and contact information including both Washington, D.C., and home state offices, addresses, telephone numbers, and e-mail addresses. The school librarian will immediately think of introducing students to the Government Printing Office publication *Congressional Directory* (print or online; www.gpoaccess.gov/cdirectory/index.html) but will probably suggest that students also investigate the *Congressional Pictorial Directory* (same website), and possibly, if working with younger students, *Ben's Guide to U.S. Government*, also at the same GPO website. Another good source of information is the Congressional Quarterly publication *Washington Information Directory* (www.cqpress.com/product/Washington-Information-Directory-Online.html). Many of the older, standard print reference sources, such as the multi-volume *Dictionary of American Biography*, are limited to those notable Americans (including members of the U.S. Congress) who have "passed on." The research and narrative in these works are excellent, of course, but would not include a sitting congressperson. *Who's Who in America* and *Who's Who in American Politics* (www.marquis-whoswho.com) would be appropriate print or online sources as well, though, like *Congressional Quarterly* publications, they are fairly expensive. The savvy searcher will of course check for the availability of online resources such as *Biographical Directory of the U.S. Congress*, which may be available through school, public, or academic libraries. Naturally, students will want to search the school's OPAC for in-house biographies and resources, as well as available research and periodical databases (GaleNet, EBSCO, etc.). One would expect that most congressional representatives would have personal websites, presenting an excellent opportunity to help students understand that information should always be evaluated in terms of source, timeliness, and accuracy.

As an example, students coming to the media center are in a health care track or career program in the school and are looking for information regarding the most recent food safety scare. Let's say it's peanut butter. The classroom teacher and media specialist will have collaborated to identify specific questions that the students are to investigate. Questions might include basic information about where peanut butter comes from and methods used to process the raw material for the grocery store and home, recent instances of product manufacture and possible contamination, effects of contamination on human beings, the number of humans affected, and so forth. The media specialist will want students to first investigate the school library media center resources, using the OPAC to investigate "food safety," "food and drug administration," and more specific terms such as "salmonella" or "peanut butter." Print or online encyclopedias will be used for basic definitions of terms. Online researching should include such sources as publications from the U.S. Department of Agriculture, U.S. Food and Drug Administration, MEDLINE, and other resources from the National Library of Medicine (www.nlm.nih.gov), as well as periodical databases and possibly pre-identified websites.

In chapter 3, a mention was made of a building trades instructor in a career academy high school in Florida who actively collaborated with the academic history and English teachers, with good results. Students gained academically in reading, writing, and research skills, which resulted in a better understanding of building construction history and current standards and construction materials and techniques. The school librarian can be a part of this collaboration by ensuring that students are familiar with the variety of U.S. government publications and websites pertinent to the construction and building trades, as well as publications and websites of publishing houses such as Ferguson Publishing, Cambridge Educational, Films for the Humanities & Sciences, Prentice-Hall School, and many others. Specific resources, titles, and websites will be discussed in greater detail in chapter 8. Because many of the resources are targeted to a fairly small audience, they are not necessarily regularly reviewed in selection tools such as *Booklist* and *School Library Journal.*

Collaboration with CTE instructors is essential for the school librarian in identifying material and resources of value to the student and the curriculum. Once those collaborative bridges are constructed, it becomes a relatively simple task to work with students in order to assist them in identifying specific information or technology needs for an assignment; locating resources to address those needs; assessing the pertinence of specific resources; incorporating information from those resources into the research assignment; producing a final written, visual, or oral product; and evaluating the results of their work.

Remember the line from the song "Rock Island" in the old movie musical *The Music Man*? The one that goes, "Ya gotta know the territory"? In the re-designed high school, "Ya gotta know the curriculum."

References

American Library Association. *Information Power: Building Partnerships for Learning*, 1998.

Eisenberg, M. B., and Berkowitz, R. E. *Information Problem Solving: The Big Six Skills Approach to Library and Information Skills Instruction*. Norwood, NJ: Ablex, 1988.

Elbe, Kenneth. *The Craft of Teaching*. San Francisco: Jossey-Bass Publishers, 1976.

Marquis Who's Who. Available from http://www.marquiswhoswho.com (accessed 22 August 2007).

National Forum on Information Literacy. "Definitions, Standards, and Competencies Related to Information Literacy." Available from http://www.infolit.org/definitions.html (accessed 22 August 2007).

———. "Publications." Available from http://www.infolit.org/resources.html (accessed 22 August 2007).

Partnership for 21st Century Skills. *Are They Really Ready to Work?* Available from http://www.21stcenturyskills.org/documents/FINAL_REPORT_PDF09-29-06.pdf (accessed 22 August 2007).

———. "Results That Matter: 21st Century Skills and High School Reform." Available from http://www.21stcenturyskills.org/index.php?option=com_content&task=view&id=204&Ite (accessed 22 August 2007).

SREB EvaluTech. "21st Century Skills and Information and Communications Technologies Literacy: from *A Nation at Risk* to ICT Literacy." Available from http://www.evalutech.sreb.org/21stcentury/LiteracySkills.asp (accessed 22 August 2007).

U.S. Government Printing Office. *Congressional Directory.* GPO Access. Available from http://www.gpoaccess.gov/cdirectory/index.html (accessed 22 August 2007).

"Washington Information Directory Online Edition." CQ Press. Available from http://www.cqupress.com/product/Washington-Information-Directory-Online.html (accessed 23 August 2007).

Wilson, Meredith. *The Music Man*. 1957.

6
Resources to Meet the Needs of the CTE Curriculum

"Many believe that the genius of the future, the person who can do the most, will not be the one with the best memory but the one who has access to the most information and who is able to call upon this database to solve problems."

Beth Lazerick, "Facing the Future: One School's Commitment to Computer Education"

In shaping the necessary resources and collections for the re-designed high school, the school librarian will need to rely upon knowledge of institutions and agencies outside of the school itself. As academic curricula become more stringent, and as CTE courses successfully incorporate increased and higher academic standards in application coursework, the library media center will need to keep pace in order to ensure that the print and non-print resources available in and through the center meet the needs of all courses offered in the building. As national education and business leaders insist that high school classes require more than "seat time" for course credit toward a diploma, as states develop detailed "standard" or "comprehensive" curricula for each class and each grade level and mandate frequent high-stakes testing at regular intervals, school library media programs must choose whether to lead, follow, or get out of the way.

Taking the lead is preferable to seeing the building library program eliminated or following blindly in others' muddy footprints. Leadership in this area will certainly include points mentioned earlier. Collection assessment, initiating collaborative strategies with CTE and new faculty in the building to ascertain specific resource needs, budgeting for additional funding to meet the needs, and then purchasing and making available those resources are of primary importance. Non-print resources, including databases, computer and video or DVD material, and good websites evaluated for their reliability and usefulness, must be a prominent component of "the plan." However, the school librarian must also be aware of community resources and support groups that can assist with awareness, fundraising, and resources. By working with the building administration, counselors, teachers, and parent groups, the savvy school librarian can build a strong program and collection of resources to meet curricular needs as well as individual student needs and interests.

High school students probably begin developing job and career interests and awareness long before they reach their freshman year of high school. The jobs and careers of parents and adult relatives and friends, elementary school job fairs or career awareness days, and television and other media are all providing information of a sort to young people. Likewise, the awareness grows that in the ever-changing electronic world in which we live, an individual may well have five to ten careers and two to three dozen jobs during their work life. Many young people realize fairly early that becoming an entertainment icon, a supermodel, or a professional athlete is not nearly as easy as it would appear, and that some education and preparation is necessary. Of course, as adults, we can all think of prominent national figures who have "made it" without any seeming preparation, work, or study. But that is another story.

In general, the school librarian is aware of many of the general career awareness and preparation resources available: of course, *Occupational Outlook Handbook* at www.bls.gov/oco (print, non-print, or both); the many Petersen's guides and Ferguson career prep titles; material from Prentice Hall School publishers, CRC Press, and others. Look also to, as mentioned earlier, the U.S. Government Printing Office and ERIC for possible lists of material for specific curricula, as well as to professional organizations and associations (look what ALA and AASL have provided in our own field). So investigate the Association for Career Technical Education (ACTE), the U.S. Department of Education's Office of Vocational and Adult Education, the Center on Education and Training for Employment, among others. Becoming familiar with professional and research organizations, with literature other than our own, will be increasingly important to the school librarian as high schools re-evaluate their curricula and programs.

Think of these organizations and associations as part of the school librarian's professional network. By establishing and maintaining ties to student, parent, and community organizations and institutions, the school librarian can be in an excellent position to access and acquire material and resources needed by students, but, perhaps more importantly, to know and refer students directly to those sources of information (human or otherwise).

Meeting the information needs of the high school student who will not be going directly (if at all) to college requires that the school librarian understand and develop good working relationships with students' parents, friends, and families; with school- and community-based student groups; with the school's PTA group; with school counselors and administrative staff. School Career Days are important events to monitor, as are student part-time and summer job opportunities in the community.

Lukenbill's *Community Resources in the School Library Media Center: Concepts and Methods* (2004) provides a look at a British model for developing a catalog or database of local community agencies, special interest groups, and individuals of potential value to the school. Such a database can provide contact information for faculty and student groups interested in classroom speakers or speakers and programs for student organizations. In addition, for the school librarian, it can connect individuals to specialized information and access to resources of interest to the high school student body.

Universities across the country are investigating and implementing "service learning" courses and undergraduate and graduate assignments or projects that involve student work in school and community projects. While numbers of these service learning projects involve landscaping, painting buildings or rooms, as well as the construction, refurbishing, or renovating of playground equipment, with the end result being student learning as well as accomplishing school goals of positive community interface, there are other possibilities that hold the promise of greater application of academic content. High schools that do encourage volunteerism and service learning among options for students will find that, at the very least, students are learning about jobs and careers that they may not have previously considered.

Career academy-type programs encourage student "hands-on" work that reinforces academic preparation. Consider high school building trades projects in which students plan and construct storage sheds or even small houses that are then sold to fund the purchase of materials for the next semester or school year project. A wonderful older video, no longer available, sponsored in part by AASL titled *You Know It: Building with Information,* details the activities of a group of high school students embarking on just such a project. For projects such as this, students need access to information about building and safety codes and local zoning regulations among many other specifics. It should be possible for the library media program to take the lead in making this type of information available, and to facilitate its access and use by students.

Local professional and service organizations can be a strong area of support for the re-designed high school and a source of information for the school librarian in that they may be able to pinpoint specific resources or types of resources that should be available to high school students interested in particular career areas. The Rotarians, Lions, Kiwanis, Elks, and many others are active in supporting public education and may be of assistance in identifying community employment opportunities and the expectations that these potential employers have for new, first-time employees. If local employers follow national reports and trends, they want to hire young people who are literate and math-wise, who are personable and articulate and willing to work at entry-level jobs to learn about the business. If this is the case in your local area, it is wise to look for and purchase material on preparing resumes and developing interview skills, and for assisting students in investigating local businesses and employment opportunities for their specific and particular needs and requirements.

If they exist in your community, trade unions can be a good way to identify resources needed or required in apprenticeship or training programs that they run or support. While the school librarian may hesitate to purchase expensive text materials for such programs, knowledge of supplemental material can be very useful for both the library media program and the students. Trade unions and local chambers of commerce are both good sources of information about local employment possibilities. Another possible source is the U.S. Department of Labor, Bureau of Labor Statistics (www.bls.gov), State and Local Employment, and the U.S. Bureau of the Census (www.census.gov) area profile for your community. A sure knowledge of local employment and educational opportunities should help the school librarian immeasurably in identifying standard and newly published material of value to current students.

Other resources for the school librarian to explore are the majors and career tracks available at area community colleges, industrial and trade schools, and vocational and technical institutes. An awareness of these programs or majors will allow the school librarian to locate and purchase material appropriate to preparation for those career tracks. Most post–high school institutions will have library media centers with collections designed to support the curricula of their particular programs. Developing a good working relationship with peers in these institutions will likewise be an invaluable aid, as a means of sharing information about new or appropriate resources for the re-designed high school library.

As the keynote speaker at the 2007 AASL conference in Reno, Nevada, Dan Pink quoted the superintendent of the Fairfax, Virginia, public school system as saying, "We need to prepare kids for their future, not our past." Pink (author of *A Whole New Mind*, 2005) noted also that routine work is disappearing, replaced by machines capable not only of lifting heavy loads, but of performing nearly instantaneous calculations, and tutoring humans in step-by-step, right answer/wrong answer, mass production preparation for tests and exams. High tech, according to Pink, is a means rather than an end.

For the school librarian in the re-designed high school, that means an increased awareness of the needs of the workplace of tomorrow, and a strong working relationship with CTE, community and technical college, and trade and vocational school faculty and staff to understand the information needs of students today. Particular attention should be paid to changing curricula and new classes and courses as they are developed. Colleges offer majors in designing computer games. Community colleges prepare students for careers in the justice system with AA degrees. JROTC in high schools focus young people on opportunities and careers in the military. Business programs in high schools provide entry-level opportunities in secretarial, clerical, and bookkeeping fields. The school librarian must know and understand the high school curriculum and the opportunities it presents for students, as well as career preparation opportunities in other local area institutions.

Analyze the curriculum, collaborate with the faculty, do continuing collection assessment, and prepare careful budget documents that explain and justify the need for new print and non-print material to support the school's "forgotten half." Then, you will be prepared to market, or sell, the library media program to the entire high school population.

References

Danielson, J. *You Know It: Building with Information*. VHS. Lincoln, NE: GPN Productions, 1998.

Lazerick, Beth. "Facing the Future: One School's Commitment to Computer Education." *Top of the News* (Spring 1983): 262.

Lukenbill, W. Bernard. *Community Resources in the School Library Media Center: Concepts and Methods*. Westport, CT: Libraries Unlimited, 2004.

Pink, Daniel. *A Whole New Mind: Moving from the Information Age to the Conceptual Age*. New York: Riverhead Books, 2005.

U.S. Department of Labor, Bureau of Labor Statistics. *Occupational Outlook Handbook, 2006–07 Edition*. Available from http://www.bls.gov/oco/ (accessed 15 November 2007).

7
Reaching Out: To Market, To Market

"As a general rule, the most successful man in life is the man with the best information."

Benjamin Disraeli

Marketing the library media program and its resources to faculty and students in career focus and CTE areas might initially appear to be very challenging. Actually, it probably will be very challenging, because in so many instances, the school librarian simply is not familiar with the programs and curricula of the re-designed school and the needs of the school-to-work student. However, the process for developing awareness for the resources and services of the library media program among students and faculty in career and CTE areas is absolutely no different than developing awareness of resources and services for additional Advanced Placement or International Baccalaureate or other academic course areas.

There continue to be three primary foci for any type of library program:

✧ Select and acquire information resources pertinent to the needs of the institution.

✧ Organize and arrange that information in such a manner that it is easily available to the constituents.

✧ Instruct and assist users in accessing and evaluating that information for their specific needs.

These foci are, and have been, addressed by the American Library Association, American Association of School Librarians, National Council for the Accreditation of Teacher Education, and National Board for Professional Teacher Standards in their identification of the roles of the school librarian, and in descriptions of what the school librarian should know and be able to do. As we are all aware, *Information Power* (ALA, 1998, 4–5) describes these roles as being that of

❖ Teacher

❖ Instructional Partner

❖ Information Specialist

❖ Program Administrator

Patterned to some extent on these identified roles, the *ALA/AASL Standards for Initial Programs for School Library Media Specialist Preparation* (www.ala.org/ala/aasl/aasleducation/schoollibrarymed/ala-aasl_slms 2003.pdf) identifies four specific program standards for institutions involved in preparing school library media specialists. These standards describe what school librarians should know and be able to do:

Standard 1: Use of Information and Ideas

Efficient and Ethical Information-Seeking Behavior

Literacy and Reading

Access to Information

Stimulating Learning Environment

Standard 2: Teaching and Learning

Knowledge of Learners and Learning

Effective and Knowledgeable Teacher

Information Literacy Curriculum

Standard 3: Collaboration and Leadership

Connection with the Library Community

Instructional Partner

Educational Leader

Standard 4: Program Administration

Managing Information Resources: Selecting, Organizing, Using

Managing Program Resources: Human, Financial, Physical

Comprehensive and Collaborative Strategic Planning and Assessment

Each standard and each point within each standard is accompanied by a simple rubric detailing Unacceptable, Acceptable, and Target goals; Supporting Explanations; and Representative Evidence statements. For instance, in Standard 1: Use of Information and Ideas, one statement of supporting explanation says: "School library media candidates model efficient and ethical information-seeking strategies. Possessing these skills will enable school librarians to provide information in response to the needs of the school community, and to help learners articulate their information needs" (11–12). One of the points of representative evidence for this same Standard 1 states that " ... documents: demonstrating wide knowledge of children and young adult literature; showing an understanding of ethical use of materials; showing ways to effectively use ideas and information i.e. bibliographies, projects, events, promotional materials, web tutorials or website designs."

The *NBPTS Library Media Standards* (www.nbpts.org), in a manner similar to that of the ALA/AASL/NCATE guidelines, attempts to define what school librarians know and are able to do. NBPTS outlines three broad categories, which encompass ten standards (7–43).

What Library Media Specialists Know

Standard I:	Knowledge of Learners
Standard II:	Knowledge of Teaching and Learning
Standard III:	Knowledge of Library and Information Studies

What Library Media Specialists Do

Standard IV:	Integrating Instruction
Standard V:	Leading Innovation through the Library Media Program
Standard VI:	Administering the Library Media Program

How Library Media Specialists Grow as Professionals

Standard VII:	Reflective Practice
Standard VIII:	Professional Growth
Standard IX:	Ethics, Equity, and Diversity
Standard X:	Leadership, Advocacy, and Community

Partnerships

Publicizing, marketing, and developing outreach and advocacy strategies for the library media specialist involved in re-design will require a knowledge of the form that high school re-design is taking in your state, your district, and your high school. Two national agencies that track re-design efforts are the National Conference of State Legislatures (www.ncsl.org/programs/educ/HSReform.htm) and the Council of Chief State School Officers (CCSSO; www.ccsso.org/projects/State_Strategies_to_Redesign_High_Schools/State_Reports/). CCSSO provides direct web links to re-design plans for each of the 23 states (as of June 2005) that had completed and filed such plans, as well as a "State Report Matrix" that reports on states' attention to the following "Issue Areas":

◇ Student-Centered Teaching and Learning
◇ Increasing the Value and Rigor of a High School Diploma
◇ Standards, Assessment, and Accountability
◇ P–16 (transition from pre-kindergarten through college)
◇ Taking Reform Statewide/Engaging Stakeholders

The ALA/AASL/NCATE standards specify that the school librarian should have a knowledge of teaching and learning (ALA/AASL/NCATE Standard 2: Teaching and Learning) and a specific Knowledge of Learners and Learning. NBPTS likewise ("What Library Media Specialists Know" Standard I: Knowledge of Learners") addresses the need to know and understand the student and student needs. Note the CCSSO "Issue Area" above, stressing the need for "Student Centered Teaching and Learning." "Student Centered Teaching and Learning" is another way of expressing the old "guide by the side, not a sage on a stage" method of engaging students in doing, exploring, researching, and producing, not simply sitting in orderly rows and listening.

Promoting and marketing the library media program to new components and personnel in the re-designed high school are simple and basic in outline form, though not always simple to implement. In one's mind (if not on paper), produce a simple agenda, as if preparing for a meeting of some sort. The KISS (Keep it Simple, Stupid) method is always appropriate.

I. Introductions:

When new faculty and new programs arrive in your building, make it a point to meet with the new teachers and to introduce yourself. This can be accomplished easily, by setting up a "Welcome New Faculty" reception in the library media center (with or without refreshments), by conducting a short orientation tour, or by providing a short list of general and specialized print and electronic resources that might begin to meet their needs. More importantly, however, this should be a time when you, the school librarian, listen to them. Ask questions about their programs and show interest. Take notes.

The introductory session may be the appropriate time to schedule one-on-one time with each new faculty, so that you can get a better picture of particulars of each specific new program (robotics, for instance) and individual courses that will be offered, as well as anticipated student demographics for the program. Will initial coursework be introductory, focused on ninth graders and basic concepts, or will a complete curriculum (9–12) be in place from the outset? Of course, the school librarian does not have funding to support the purchase of textbooks or highly specialized databases or necessary electronic or mechanical tools essential to each of these programs, but developing an understanding of the type of general reference and research and resource materials that would support the program is very important. Streaming video? Mathematics or testing tutorials? Automotive manuals? Young people taking classes in many of these highly technical and demanding course areas will need to be prepared to search databases, to identify and use appropriate websites, to be able to not only locate but correctly cite information and resources that they have located, and to write and read efficiently, effectively, and easily. Ensure that the classroom teacher is aware that the school librarian and program is fully prepared to work with students in developing research and documentation skills in any subject area, including the teacher's subject area, with currently available resources.

II. Old Business:

After gathering both general and specialized information about new programs and courses, schedule a short meeting time with each individual new faculty member. Prior to the meeting date and time, cumulate a short list of those resources currently available that should be of value to each teacher and his or her students. These might include information on specialized reference material such as encyclopedias of science and technology, the approximate number of print volumes in the 600s, the general or specialized databases available, the approximate number of indexed journals appropriate to the area, computer labs and scheduling information, pertinent computer programs, availability of streaming video, Internet access, the existence of the school library website, the availability of a building-wide course management system, high-tech teaching stations (computer with Internet access, projector, video/DVD capability, white-boards, etc.), subject-specific video/DVDs, magazine and journal subscriptions, and so forth. Keep it to one page. Do not do a title by title listing of the book titles that you currently have.

Let the new teachers know that you will be pleased to walk them through specific areas of the library media center at a mutually convenient time, and then make the time. Ask them to identify materials and resources they have used in the past or that they have seen at conferences or read about that are not available in your collection. Make notes, and indicate that you will check for current prices and availability.

III. New Business:

Follow through. Check the availability and prices of specific titles that may have been mentioned, and then include those in your order file and budget. Next, include those new teachers in your "routing list" of reviews of new print and non-print material that you have spotted in *Booklist*, *School Library Journal*, or other professional review sources. Ask their opinion as to the title or titles appropriate for the school collection. Plan to budget for and order those things that get thumbs up. Remember, these materials do not necessarily need to be career or job oriented. Solid fiction and non-fiction, pictorial and well-illustrated works, graphic novels, and DVD/videos all help young people to understand and appreciate concepts and subject areas. Work actively to promote and then keep the resources and services of the library media center in the spotlight for all areas of the curriculum, faculty, and students.

IV. Action Items:

Use library media center display areas to highlight the work and projects of the school-to-work, tech/prep, or career academy students. Displays of student art and photography, videos, web design, games, science projects, fashion design, agriculture projects (think roses, not cows here), and other research projects are tremendous draws to the library media center. Think about having on display in the library media center (if space permits, of course) that 1948 Harley-Davidson motorcycle that an automotive student has so carefully and painstakingly restored. Back up any student project display with appropriate print and non-print resources from your library media center. Student work of any type will be a draw for all students in the building.

Ensure that all teachers in the building are familiar with Southern Regional Education Board's "EvaluTech" (www.evalutech.sreb.org) with its Instructional Resources section, which includes Lesson Plans and other Resources, Accessible Technology for Students with Disabilities, E-Learning Software, and an online, keyword-searchable database of reviews of instructional materials. Among the Instructional Resources listed at the time of this writing, Mathematics included links to lesson plans and websites, enrichment activities, and digital libraries. Science likewise included links to lesson plans and websites, teaching strategies, a resource collection, and links to specific resources in astronomy, earth science, human growth and development, physical science, science projects and science fairs, digital libraries, and biographies. Other subject areas noted include Language Arts and Social Studies. Website links are nearly always to .gov, .edu, or .org sites.

The Educator's Reference Desk (www.eduref.org/Eric) also provides access to a wide range of educational support material, lesson plans, and resources found on various federal, state, university, non-profit, and commercial Internet sites, many of which will be of value to building-level educators. Kathy Schrock's *Discovery Education* website (http://school.discoveryeducation.com) includes teacher-developed lesson plans, but also the "Kathy Schrock's Guide for Educators." This section provides links to a vast array of websites, including agricultural education resources (which itself includes links to agricultural law, ideas for agricultural science fair projects, and an agricultural image gallery), business sources and grants, health and fitness, and technical and career education information among an alphabet of others. Some of Schrock's links lead to commercial entities, though most lead to non-profit organizations and educational and governmental entities.

Teachers in all subject areas should also be aware of *Kids.gov* (www.kids.gov), the official kids' portal for U.S. government agency websites. While focused on federal government sites specific to K–8, the "Educators" section provides links to material appropriate for adult use, such as information on careers. *Ben's Guide to U.S. Government for Kids* (http://bensguide.gpo.gov) is more specific in that it provides links to U.S. history sites, branches of government, and the legislative process, but with resources that are specific to grades 9 through 12.

In addition to database links such as these to sources of websites that have been evaluated, verified, and recommended, suggest that teachers themselves identify, evaluate, and review websites of particular value to their students and classes. The next step is to help ensure that selected sites become a part of the instructor's course management system's resource sites, or the school librarian should include them in a library link of recommended reference/resource sites for specific course areas.

The library media center website itself should promote and highlight resources and services of the center for all courses and areas of the curriculum and should be used to promote library media center resources and services as well as to inform. Consider including a monthly or quarterly highlight of a new building teacher or course, with a note on that person's favorite reading material, website, or computer game or the course description, requirements, and suggested reading. Another possibility for many schools might be the use of the library media center's blog or wiki to highlight individual departments or curriculum areas on a rotating basis, with teachers responsible for writing about their classes and themselves, and, of course, favorite books, magazines, films, computer/video games, music, and so forth. Provide teachers an opportunity to be in the whole school spotlight, courtesy of the library media center.

Deborah Levitov (2007) writes of advocacy as being the means or process of figuring out how to get others to take on the cause and speak for the library media center. She refers to using reading promotions (29) as a means of public relations for her library media center, a way of getting students, teachers, and parents connected to the media center. If others—administrators, teachers, and students—buy in to the library media center and advocate and support its program and budget, you will have succeeded in marketing your agency.

Marketing the library media center in the re-designed high school means reaching out to find out about new courses and classes and faculty, and evaluating the library media center resources and services in respect to these newly identified needs. Be prepared to work closely with the new subject specialty teachers to identify new materials, and be prepared to work with their students to ensure that each is competent in evaluating sources of information appropriate to their individual need and interest, locating that information, and using that information in an ethical manner. You, the school librarian, are now exemplifying the roles of Teacher, Instructional Partner, Information Specialist, and Program Administrator by marketing to the new elements in your re-designed high school.

The next question is: How do you, the school librarian, take on this additional responsibility for working with new faculty and curricular areas when you are currently poorly staffed and funded?

References

American Association of School Librarians. *ALA/AASL Standards for Initial Programs for School Library Media Specialist Preparation*. Available from http://www.ala.org/ala/aasl/aasleducation/schoollibrarymed/ala-aasl_slms 2003.pdf (accessed 13 December 2007).

Ben's Guide to U.S. Government for Kids. Available from http://bensguide.gpo.gov (accessed 13 December 2007).

Council of Chief State School Officers. High School Redesign State Reports. Available from http://www.ccsso.org/projects/State_Strategies_Redesign_High_ Schools/State_Reports/ (accessed 13 December 2007).

Eble, Kenneth E. *The Craft of Teaching: A Guide to Mastering the Professor's Art*. San Francisco: Jossey-Bass, 1994.

The Educator's Reference Desk: Search GEM/ERIC. Available from http://www. eduref.org/Eric (accessed 13 December 2007).

"EvaluTech." Southern Regional Education Board. Available from http://www. evalutech.sreb.org (accessed 13 December 2007).*Information Power*. Chicago: American Libraries Association, 1998.

Kids.gov. Available from http://kids.gov/ (accessed 13 December 2007).

Levitov, Deborah. *Knowledge Quest* 36, no. 1 (2007): 29.Nation Conference of State Legislatures. "High School Reform Overview." Available from http://www. ncsl.org/programs/educ/HSReform.htm (accessed 13 December 2007).

National Board for Professional Teaching Standards. Available from http://www. nbpts.org/ (accessed 13 December 2007).

Schrock, Kathy. "Kathy Schrock's Guide for Educators." *Discovery Education*. Available from http://school.discoveryeducation.com/schrockguide/ (accessed 13 December 2007).

8
Planning and Organization for the Re-Designed High School Library

"... Obviously folks not on the front line of schools don't realize the teaching that the school librarian does.... They see only the classroom model and are unaware of how much connection the real live library person has with her clients. The information management skills she teaches last a lifetime, unlike some of the more esoteric pieces of information conveyed in classrooms, which have the half-life of a fruit fly (or until the next test)."

Diane Noble, personal e-mail message, April 8, 1997

Teacher, Instructional Partner, Information Specialist, and Program Administrator are roles advocated by the American Association of School Librarians (AASL) in *Information Power* (1998, 4–5) and with the National Council for Accreditation of Teacher Education (NCATE) in the *ALA/ AASL Standards for Initial Programs for School Library Media Specialist Preparation* (under revision as of 2007), as well as the National Board for Professional Teaching Standards (NBPTS) *Library Media Standards* (www.nbpts.org). The newly released *Standards for the 21st Century Learner* (American Association of School Librarians, 2007, available at http://www.ala.org/aasl/standards) addresses the learning and information skills necessary to enable all of today's students to succeed in the workplaces of tomorrow and the near future. These standards rely upon the skills of the school librarian as teacher, partner, and researcher. The role of program administrator is not specifically addressed in these new standards, though that role is implied and underlying to the other roles.

The caliber of the administration of the library media program will be of increasing importance for the CTE faculty and students in the re-designed high school. The reason for that, of course, is that if the library media program is to support all areas of the school curriculum and all students in the building, the building staff and perhaps district administration must be asked to address staffing, space, technology, and budget needs for the library media center. The school and district cannot afford to support a building program that serves well only a portion of the students in the school, and therefore must be made aware of the fiscal needs of the users of the library media center in supporting new or re-designed programs in the building.

Previous chapters of this book take note of the history of school libraries and school-to-work programs, of previous and current school reform efforts, of research in vocational and career technical education, of anticipated career opportunities for today's high school students, of post–high school technical and training programs, of information and technology skills models, of the need to assess the print and non-print collections of the library media center, and of the need to reach out and market the library media program to all students and faculty in the building. Recognizing and addressing these needs requires that the school librarian be well organized and have well-honed administrative and managerial skills. The high school librarian must also have the willingness to be or become an educational leader in the school and school district.

The library media program will not become the information center of the entire school and all of its students without the energy and drive and organization of the library media center staff. The steps to achieving this goal involve research, collection and services assessment, budgeting, marketing, and selling the resources and services of the library media center. Going back to school for a master's of business administration (MBA) is not a realistic option for most school librarians. That degree would, of course, provide a window to the vocabulary and methodologies of the commercial business world, but would perhaps not shed much light on an understanding of student learning styles and information needs for tomorrow's job market.

The school librarian must be willing to investigate and understand the changing needs of the re-designed high school curriculum and the CTE or school-to-work student. As information professionals, we may not be directly involved in planning an expanded CTE program or in other areas of curriculum design. However, practitioners in library media centers must know the high school completion and dropout rates for their district and their specific school and the ways that school and district administrators are re-designing curriculum and classes or developing new programs that will appeal to and involve students in their own education and hence their own futures. It is a certainty today that young people *must* have a high school diploma to succeed in nearly any employment endeavor. The school librarian must know and understand state and local plans to re-design high school curricula to better meet the needs of the non-college bound student, as well as be or become familiar with the local area job market. School librarians must exhibit an understanding of their individual school demographics and curricula. That's step one, the demographic and curriculum research phase.

Step two involves, of course, the assessment of the current library media center collection and resources. Is the collection geared primarily to the college bound? Are all (or the majority) of the students in the high school expected to attend college? If the answer to the first question is yes, and the answer to the second question is no, the school librarian needs to take a hard look at the amount of material in the collection focused on the analysis of the works of Shakespeare or nineteenth-century British poetry and consider the age and condition of material dealing with science, technology, and health care, not to mention the arts and humanities. What databases and computer programs and other non-print materials are available? What is the focus of those particular resources in terms of curricular specificity? Are existing computer labs and programs adequate to the needs of expanded and specialized student needs? Does the school have closed circuit television? Are television/video/film production facilities a possibility? The library media center staff must be involved in plans to develop any new programs, in order to provide necessary print and non-print resources to support those programs.

With an assessment of the current building print and non-print information resources, facilities, and technologies available, the school librarian can begin to gather data for a long-range budget document or long-range plan (step three) that will allow for either the development or the purchase of resources and facilities that will better meet the needs of all students and emerging programs in the building. Long-term plans should also reflect an awareness of future professional and clerical staffing needs of the library media center, as well as changing facility and technical resource requirements. A long-range budget or planning document reflects both knowledge of curriculum and faculty and student requirements, but also serves as a marketing tool for the library media program. A good, well-developed budget and planning document tells building administration, department heads, and faculty that the school librarian is aware of or willing to learn about all student and faculty information needs that exist in or are planned for the building, and that the school librarian is able and willing to work closely with all faculty members and students to identify and acquire any new specific resources and services needed for existing or developing programs. This means, of course, that the library media center program and budget documents will more likely have the support of all departments and programs within the school. As Deborah Levitov (2007) wrote, "advocacy" is about involving others in speaking for and supporting the library media center program and resources. If the budget plan for the school library media center provides indication of support for all programs, including CTE in the building, faculty will in turn support the budget and the library media center program itself.

The short-term or annual budget document prepared by the school librarian should likewise involve working with classroom teachers and program advocates for every curricular and activities area for their suggestions and recommendations for the purchase of specific material and resources.

In theory the building-level library media center program budget is supported with adequate and regularly allotted funding from the district and the state. In reality this funding, when it exists, is frequently not sufficient to provide necessary information and a good variety of leisure reading resources for all programs and students. School librarians all too often find themselves in the position of fundraisers in order to support the purchase of even basic resources necessary to the various educational programs in the building. With the average cost of a single book for the high school library now exceeding $20.00, many schools do not have the funds to purchase even one new book per student per year. Expensive but necessary reference material (for instance, the *National Electrical Code 2005* [softcover version] is currently priced at $75.00) may be highly desirable for schools with building trades and other CTE programs but not easily affordable. An alternative to selling candy, pencils, or ID cards might be exploring the options for grant funding. Grant money may be available on a one-time basis only, so the school librarian would be wise to regard it as "start-up" funding to purchase resources needed to support new or newly expanded CTE programs.

Grant funding for resources for the library media center program in support of CTE classes may be available from sources outside the school or district. The Carl D. Perkins Career and Technical Education Act (reauthorized in 2006) makes federal monies available to state departments of education for career and technical education programs in each state. State departments of education then disperse the funding to local school districts and technical training programs. The Perkins Act is briefly summarized by the Association for Career and Technical Education at http://www. acteonline.org/policy/legislative_issues/Perkins_background.cfm. Working collaboratively with CTE faculty to request funding or write a grant for these federal funds to be used to purchase resources for the library media center would certainly be viewed favorably by the CTE program as a whole.

Writing grants to federal agencies such as the National Endowment for the Humanities' "Grants for Teaching and Learning Resources and Curriculum Development" (http://www.neh.gov), the National Endowment for the Arts (http://www.nea.gov), the National Institutes of Health (http://www.nih.gov), or the National Science Foundation (http://www.nsf.gov), for funding to purchase resources for the library media center program is not usually feasible for the school librarian. However, the school librarian might want to explore the variety of state and/or local chapters of these and other federal agencies for grant funding that may be available for the purchase of resources to support specific programs in the school, including the emerging CTE curriculum areas. Federal grant funding available to support the purchase of library media center materials and resources is available through the U.S. Department of Education's "Improving Literacy through School Libraries" (www.ed.gov/programs/lsl/index.html) competitive grants program. School districts qualified to apply for this funding must have at least 20 percent of the families in the district below the poverty level, as determined by the U.S. Bureau of the Census. Though not federal, the Laura Bush Foundation for America's Libraries also makes grant funding available for print materials for libraries in schools in which

90 percent or more of the students qualify for free or reduced lunches. The ALA and its divisions, including the AASL, offers a few competitive grants and awards that may be used for the purchase of resources and materials, though most are offered in support of individuals who have demonstrated exceptional service to the profession.

Some states make funding available to library media center resources through their own (not federal and not private) grant programs. An example of this might be the State of Louisiana Board of Elementary and Secondary Education's Louisiana Quality Education Support Fund, known as 8(g) grants (http://www.doe.state.la.us/lde/bese/1019.html).

State and local funding for library media center resources from non-education sources might be available through the kind of professional and business organizations noted in chapter 6. The state building trades organization perhaps, or trade unions supportive of public education initiatives in school-to-work programs could become allies in supplying start-up funding for library media center resources specific to CTE programs in that school.

Working collaboratively with teachers in all areas to solicit specific title requests, and developing an understanding of long-term program needs and goals will also enable the school librarian to develop ways of highlighting and displaying student work and accomplishments within the library media center, work that was stimulated in or by the various CTE courses and programs. Displaying and highlighting student accomplishment of any type through the library media program is positive for the students, for parents, for faculty, for building administrators, and ultimately for the school library media center.

The 19 state studies that have been completed to date linking student academic achievement to the presence of strong school library media programs with professionally trained and state-certified school library media specialists (*School Libraries Work!* 2008) do not speak specifically to the school-to-work or career technical education student, nor to that segment of young people who comprise our forgotten half. No proof, no research exists to demonstrate that the strong school library media center program with its myriad resources and professionally trained library media center staff prevents students from leaving high school before graduation. However, by reaching out to provide resources and services to courses and programs in the school that involve students in authentic learning situations, the school librarian is at the very least affecting student attitudes toward literacy, learning, and school itself.

Brandsford, Pellegrino, and Donovan (1999) wrote, "Authentic learning implies several things: that learning be centered around authentic tasks, that learning be guided with teacher scaffolding, that students be engaged in exploration and inquiry, that students have opportunities for social discourse, and that ample resources be available to students as they pursue meaningful problems. Advocates of authentic learning believe these elements support natural learning, and many of these ideals are based in theory and research on learning and cognition."

The school librarian is in a unique position and in a unique period of time to directly influence a new generation of learners. The so-called forgotten half may well not be continuing their immediate education beyond high school. In some parts of the country, even completing high school graduation requirements is a challenge. But national and state leaders, educators, business and professional people, and military leaders continue to call for meaningful high school reform that will involve preparing today's students for tomorrow's workplace and tomorrow's jobs. That means, as every new report critical of the education system has stated, that students today need math and science and certainly reading and writing skills, but they also need critical thinking and problem-solving and evaluation and research skills. Those skills comprise the school librarian's areas of greatest expertise. We teach information literacy and research and website/media evaluation. We also provide (or can and should be providing) a wide array of print and non-print resources of interest to every student in our schools, and of value to every area of the curriculum.

We must realize that most of the students who graduate from most of our public high schools will not be entering a program of higher education immediately upon completion of high school. They, even more than the immediate university-bound student, need our particular attention and instructional expertise. We will have to reach out to them, of course, in part because they may not realize how welcome they are in our libraries, and in part because they may not believe that we have services and resources and materials that they will find useful and that they will enjoy. We need to take the time and make the effort. These students are the ones who will be voting for public officials, who will be administering a good many of our resources, who will be providing information and entertainment, and who will be managing and repairing our transportation and communication industries. We need to support them now, so that they will be inclined to support us in the future.

References

American Association of School Librarians. *ALA/AASL Standards for Initial Programs for School Library Media Specialist Preparation.* Available from http://www.ala.org/ala/aasl/aasleducation/schoollibrarymed/ala-aasl_slms 2003.pdf (accessed 13 December 2007).

———. *Standards for the 21st Century Learner.* Available from http://www.ala.org/ aasl/standards (accessed 13 December 2007).

"Authentic Learning." *Visible Knowledge Project Glossary.* Available from http:// crossroads.georgetown.edu/vkp/resources/glossary/authenticlearning.htm (accessed 13 December 2007).

Brandsford, John D., James W. Pellegrino, and Suzanne Donovan. *How People Learn: Bridging Research and Practice.* Washington, DC: National Academy Press, 1999.

Information Power. Chicago: American Libraries Association, 1998.

Levitov, Deborah. *Knowledge Quest* 36, no. 1 (2007): 29.

Louisiana Department of Education. "The Louisiana Quality Education Support Fund—8(g)BESE Elementary and Secondary Education Grants." Available from http://www.doe.state.la.us/lde/bese/1019.html (accessed 13 December 2007).

National Board for Professional Teaching Standards. Available from http://www.nbpts.org (accessed 13 December 2007).

National Endowment for the Arts. Available from http://www.nea.gov (accessed 13 December 2007).

National Endowment for the Humanities. Available from http://www.neh.gov (accessed 13 December 2007).

National Institutes of Health. Available from http://www.nih.gov (accessed 13 December 2007).

National Science Foundation. Available from http://www.nsf.gov (accessed 13 December 2007).

"Perkins: Background." *ACTE Online*. Available from http://www.acteonline.org/policy/legislative_issues/Perkins_background.cfm (accessed 13 December 2007).

School Libraries Work! Scholastic Publishing. Available from http://www2.scholastic.com/content/collateral_resources/pdf/s/slw3_2008.pdf (accessed 13 December 2007).

U.S. Department of Education. "Improving Literacy through School Libraries." Available from http://www.ed.gov/programs/lsl (accessed 13 December 2007).

Index

About the Author

MARGIE J. KLINK THOMAS holds a BA degree in History from Florida State University, an MS degree in Library Science from Columbia University, and a Ph.D. in Library and Information Science from Florida State University. She lives in Baton Rouge, Louisiana, where she teaches and researches in the School of Library and Information Science at Louisiana State University.